# The Rise of Thana-Capitalism and Tourism

We live in a society that is bombarded by news of accidents, disasters and terrorist attacks. We are obsessed by the presence of death. It is commodified in newspapers, the media, entertainment and in our cultural consumption.

This book explores the notion of an emergent class of "death-seekers" who consume the spectacle of the disaster, exploring spaces of mass death and suffering. Sites that are obliterated by disasters or tragic events are recycled and visually consumed by an international audience, creating a death-seekers economy. The quest for the suffering of others allows for a much deeper reinterpretation of life, and has captivated the attention of many tourists, visiting sites such as concentration camps, disasters zones, abandoned prisons, and areas hit by terrorism. This book explores the notion of the death-seekers economy, drawing on the premise that the society of risk as imagined by postmodern sociology sets the pace to a new society: thana-capitalism. The chapters dissect our fascination with other's suffering, what this means for our own perceptions of the self, and as a tourist activity. It also explores the notion of an economy of impotence, where citizens feel the world is out of control.

This compelling book will be interest to students and scholars researching dark tourism, tourist behaviour, disaster studies, cultural studies and sociology.

**Maximiliano E. Korstanje** is Reader at the Department of Economics, University of Palermo, Argentina and a member of the Tourism Crisis Management Institute (University of Florida), the Centre for Ethnicity and Racism Studies (University of Leeds), The Forge (University of Lancaster and University of Leeds, UK) and The International Society for Philosophers, hosted in Sheffield, UK. He is Editor in Chief of *The International Journal of Safety and Security in Tourism* and *The International Journal of Cyber Warfare and Terrorism*. With more than 800 published papers and 35 books, Maximiliano E. Korstanje was nominated for five honorary doctorates for his contributions to the study of the effects of terrorism in tourism. In 2015 he became Visiting Research Fellow at the School of Sociology and Social Policy, University of Leeds, UK.

# The Rise of Thana-Capitalism and Tourism

Maximiliano E. Korstanje

Routledge
Taylor & Francis Group

LONDON AND NEW YORK

First published 2017
by Routledge
2 Park Square, Milton Park, Abingdon, Oxon OX14 4RN

and by Routledge
711 Third Avenue, New York, NY 10017

*Routledge is an imprint of the Taylor & Francis Group, an informa business*

*British Library Cataloguing in Publication Data*
A catalogue record for this book is available from the British Library

*Library of Congress Cataloging in Publication Data*
A catalog record for this book has been requested

ISBN: 978-1-138-20926-8 (hbk)
ISBN: 978-1-315-45749-9 (ebk)

Typeset in Times New Roman
by diacriTech, chennai

Printed and bound by CPI Group (UK) Ltd, Croydon, CR0 4YY

# Contents

# Preface: The Cult to Individualism

Undoubtedly, we cannot start a book that takes a central figure from narcissism without discussing the classic work by Christopher Lasch, *The Culture of Narcissism*. In this seminal text, Lasch discusses the sentiment of "despair" as a main indicator of the narcissist spirit. The question whether Westerners face a crisis of meaning in their lives, happens simply because narcissist culture does not develop any interest for the future nor the past.

"In a narcissist society—a society that gives increasing prominence and encouragement to narcissist traits—the cultural devaluation of the past reflects not only the poverty of the prevailing ideologies, which have lost their grip in reality and abandoned the attempt to master it, but the poverty of the narcissist inner life." (Lasch, xvii)

Instead of contemplating the past as something of worth which helps understand the future, narcissists always move in the present, surfing through the sensual world of desires. The psychological man of narcissist culture has replaced tradition by substitutive mechanisms as therapy or "mental health." In this line, Lasch realizes that these radical shifts derived from a collective mood that leads toward individualism, which is transforming the tenets of American society. In this context, the view of others is of paramount important to connect with an emptied inner life.

"Narcissism represents the psychological dimension of this dependence. Notwithstanding, his occasional illusions of omnipotence, the narcissist depends on others to validate his self-esteem. He cannot live without an admiring audience. His apparent freedom from family ties and industrial constraints does not free him to stand alone or to glory in his individuality." (p 10).

In retrospect, the external world that is described in literature has become in a cultural entertainment, where writers did not look to convince readers, since they only want to tell a convincingly fiction in order to escape from reality. A story which is not completely true is one of the striking aspects audience valorize in the culture of narcissism. Not surprisingly, Americans prioritize the consumption of movies over novels or other literary genres. The instantaneity and immediacy of news have replaced other social values as trust or traditional rites. Lasch starts from the premise that the subject sacrifices the inner world to embrace what happens in other environments, what the Other feels or hopes. Whether under normal conditions this belief would be positive because it produces reciprocity, Lasch exerts a radical criticism to other scholars who had delved into the individualism of the United States. As he sees it, the problem is deep-seated, enrooted in the social scaffolding of modernity. In fact, selfish lay-citizens have developed a radical disinterest in the Other, except what is conducive to individual goals. Individualism, though important, is not enough to describe the changes American character is suffering. Rather, personality seems to be the results of those values, hopes, and traits running through the culture. Following the legacy of founding parents of sociology, Lasch understands that "a narcissist personality" derives from a narcissist culture which was encouraged by the modern capitalism in America. The narcissist culture promotes not only rapid sources of gratification, consumption, and hedonism, it triggers an unbridled competence in others to be enthralled in the hall of glory. Instead of cooperating with neighbours and colleagues to reach self-achievement, citizens impeded of personal achievements feel happy for the failure of others. This suggests that not only economy but also politics face serious shifts in their content. Contemporary narcissism escapes to what has been written in the clinical literature, Lasch adds. Therefore, an acute diagnosis of American society is not only needed, but is necessary to help in an understanding capitalism at all. It is affected and affects our daily relations, the ties between parents and children as well as the ontological security developed once those children grow up. Those who in a quest for immediate gratification leave their children without protection surely were treated in the same way. From generation to generation, patterns of behaviour are replicated following a nexus between parents and children. This belief is vital in Lasch's account because it assumes that narcissism, far from being a specific pathology, can be replicated within society to form a social character. In this respect, his main thesis is that narcissists charm others to self-devaluate their ego, while producing a grandiose self that leads to a climate of further insecurity. The problem lies in the contrasting feeling developed for children towards their caretakers.

> "A child who feels so gravely threatened by his own aggressive feelings (projected onto other sand the internalized again as inner monsters) attempts to compensate himself for his experience of rage and envy with fantasies of wealth, beauty, and omnipotence. These fantasies, together with the internalized images of the good parents with which he attempts to defend himself, become the core of 'grandiose conception of the self.'" (p 39)

Following Lasch beyond the omnipotence of narcissists, an insecure climate of existence prevails. While parents are captivated by a sensual world of struggle, consuming and self-motivation, children and an entire generation suffer a much deeper resentment against their parents sublimating into a narcissist character. This seems to be the reason why narcissism populated in the society without limits. The internalized figure of mother, or at least caretaker, plays a crucial role in the configuration of these types of psychological traits. Unlike other psychologists which situate the problem in the boundaries of individual case, Lasch acknowledges that we are witnessing a radical shift in our culture, which is producing future narcissist generations. It is unfortunate that the gap left by the troubling connection of parents and their offspring, or emptiness, is fulfilled by advertising and mass-consumption. Last but not least, managerial studies show amply how upper-managers are as not eager for wealth or achievement as in earlier decades, but in the illusion others see they are winners. The concept of loyalty is only bestowed on those who may serve as instrument to one's own goals. This instrumentality appeals to an indifference of the real suffering of others, unless by the exacerbation of self-gratifications. Indeed, at a closer look Lasch and his book ignited a cohort of studies with focus on narcissism to the extent of coming across with valid indicators that helps understand our contemporary world. Far from disappearing, these indicators have not only remained but also intensified. The culture resulted from the rise of gamesman, who is interested in using others for his purposes and avoids intimacy and ethical liability as unworthy things. This is one of the reasons why sooner or later, narcissists fail or their projects are ransacked. Basically, narcissists only feel and see the world as mirrors of themselves, which does not permeate to external events unless they bromg reflection to the inner image. Based on the myth of "success," which was widely explored by other experts, the capitalist society educates its workforce for "survival" alone. This happens because "the American cult of friendliness conceals but does not eradicate a murderous competition for goods and positions; indeed, this competition has grown more savage in an age of diminishing expectations" (p. 64). For Lasch, our propensity to consume death derives from the decomposition of a collective spirit into a new one, more closed to desire and self-gratification. News of terrorism, crime, violence, and riots is not only disseminated to all classes, but revitalizes the experience of self. Since the past no longer offers a valid guidance for people, the world becomes more unpredictable. Doubtless, Lasch pivoted in the understanding of thana-capitalism even if he never coined this term, nor deepened in the examination of thanatology. This is one of the tasks this book attempts to continue. Whatever the case may be, Lasch reminds readers that capitalism undermines the rights of people to commoditize them, where humans are limited to being exchangeable objects.

*Maximiliano E. Korstanje*
*Buenos Aires, March 23, 2016*

# Introduction

From the articles and books of Jean Baudrillard and Zygmunt Bauman, which I first came across some decades ago, I have adopted the belief that capitalism has started to change toward unknown horizons and unimagined forms. Unsure of what direction this change is heading, I have explored not only the genesis of capitalism through a radical analysis of Norse mythology (Korstanje, 2015) but also the main limitations of biopolitics. Particularly, I contended with Baudrillard, Foucault and Bauman that, while capitalism was mutating into stricter disciplinary ways, it was doing so in contradiction with their diagnoses. Over recent decades, it is true that a global audience has been captivated by the rise of an atmosphere where disasters, terrorism and virus outbreaks instilled panic into the population. In fact, the problem of ISIS and terrorism has changed geopolitics after 9/11. While terrorists planned their attacks on military targets or celebrities through the 1970s, now mobile civilians are hosted then kidnapped and decapitated in public to expand a veil of terror over many central nations. It is tempting to say that part of the influence of terrorism exerted in the Occident depends on the obsession of Westerners to consume news covering terrorist cruelty. Human suffering such as poverty and hunger, adjoined to violence, has been thematized and visually consumed in tourist circuits worldwide. As we will see in this book, large cities such as Rio de Janeiro and Bombai are visited annually by thousands of tourists who manifest their need to feel how these non-European "Others" are pressed to survive. This opens the doors to the articulation of discourses where the suffering of Others remains as the main criterion of attraction. The same applies for an uncanny custom, the visit to zones of disasters, abandoned jails or spaces of mass death and pain. Jean Baudrillard called this "the spectacle of disaster." These types of spectacles, instead of producing a pseudo-reality, appear to be conducive to tactics to control the workforce—to mitigate their potential discontent levels to be tolerated as the status quo. No less true is that terrorists saw in leisure-spots or tourist destinations fertile grounds to create political instability, in order for their claims to be accepted. Though terrorism is not the common-thread argument in this book, it is fascinating to see how the system recycles spaces of mass death, suffering and pain such as Ground Zero into a spectacle. This raises a more than interesting question that guides all my investigation: To what extent has capitalism posed death as its main cultural value?

The evolution of capitalism historically has taken many shapes. Mercantilism set the pace of industrialism, and this latter force paved the way for the rise of modern capitalism. After the accident of Chernobyl, sociologists devoted considerable effort to criticizing the role played by technology in an ever-changing world. Always under the influence of Durkheim or Weber, social scientists envisaged a new stage that turned out to be alienatory for the social fabric. Quite aside from this, sociology devoted considerable effort to understanding the world of risk as a precondition of social ties' decline; even, as the founding parents, social scientists have woefully adopted a pejorative view of modernity which in some conditions affects their diagnosis. The hopes and dreams of rational Westerners contemplated risks and threats as anomalies produced by the complex interactions of many agents and components within interconnected systems that should adapt to the environment. The precedent conception of a social world, more associated with biology, endorsed excessive trust in the possibilities of a nation-state to give protection to their citizens. The society of risk as it was imagined by Beck and Giddens, two senior sociologists who were representative of an age, understood risks as glitches which should be fixed. The globalization and the complexity of modern productive systems prevented a clear diagnosis to expand the understanding of how these glitches might be reversed. It created a paradoxical situation because the technology employed to mitigate risks reproduces the conditions for the advent of disasters, such as Chernobyl. This raises the question, do we live in an climate of fear, as Nobel Prize–winner Wole Soyinka wrote?

The decadence still visible in democracy allied with the decline of human rights results in an atmosphere of anxiety which can be broken only by ethnic tolerance and recognition of human dignity. Pungent, Soyinka's essays lead readers through the complex world of current politics, revealing Soyinka's own experience in Africa and his sense of social issues. The whole provides an understanding of terrorism-related issues. Soyinka examines qualitatively to what extent people feel more fear in spite of technical and material advances in recent decades. The preface argues that the world cannot escape social instability when perpetrators of crimes can sell their stories to the media. Latin America and Africa have experienced this state of affairs for many years. Generally, the 1970s and '80s are characterized by the advent of bloody dictatorships that silenced their dissenting voices by violence and removal of dignity. This provided the springboard for the post-9/11 events that are shocking the United States and Europe. Soyinka claims that 9/11 did not surprise him. From that moment onwards, international public opinion (even in Africa) experienced a new climate of fear, in spite of the previous experiences of political terror. Soyinka believes the world has faced extreme situations of panic before 9/11 ranging from Nazism and the Second World War to nuclear weapon testing. One of the aspects of global power that facilitates this feeling of uncertainty seems to be the lack of a visible rivalry once the USSR collapsed. The politic terror promulgated by states diminishes the dignity of enemies.

These practices are rooted inside a territory but paved the way for a new form of terrorism which ended in the World Trade Center attacks. It is incorrect to see 9/11 as the beginning of a new fear; rather, it is the latest demonstration of power exerted by a global empire over its periphery. Mass communication, though, transformed our ways of perceiving terrorism even if it did not alter the conditions that facilitate the new state of war. Unlike classical totalitarian states which are constructed by means of material asymmetries, the quasi-states construct their legitimacy by denouncing the injustices of the world. Quasi-states are not only terrorist cells but also megacorporations which work in complicity, producing weapons for one side or the other. Making profit of human suffering is a primary aspect that characterizes these quasi-states. The uncertainty these corporations engender denies the minimum codes of war by emphasizing the inexistence of boundaries and responsibilities. Once rectitude has been substituted with the right to exercise power, pathways toward a moral superiority are frustrated. Unlike the disaster of the napalm-bombing of noncombatants perpetuated by the United States in Vietnam, this new war-on-terror is characterized by targeting innocents as a primary option. In opposition to conventional wars, war-on-terror expands fear under the following two assumptions: (1) hits can take place anywhere and anytime, and (2) there are no limits to brutality inflicted on noncombatants. Wars depend on the capacity to control others based on the principle of power. Governments often need the material resources of their neighbours. Where the expropriation method of capitalist trade fails, war finds success. One might speculate that war should be understood as an extension of economic production. The role played by fear in late modernity is rooted in a desire for domination that has nothing to do with religiosity or even with religious fundamentalism, which in recent years has become synonymous with cruelty.

As a backdrop, Cass Sunstein (2002a) proposed a model to understand emotions within rational decision making. Per his viewpoint, our decisions are subject to emotional neglects that sooner or later affect our derived diagnosis. Instead of joining with populist demands, the state should use rationality to evaluate the pros and cons of social programs and risk-management plans. The worse thing officials can do is to follow the doctrine of "precautionary principle" as it was formulated in Europe. In earlier books such as *A Difficult World* (Korstanje, 2015), I have outlined the legacy of Sunstein, Beck and Giddens, but things have since gone in another direction. This new capitalism abandoned the conceptual paradigms of risk society, to make from the spectacle of disaster its main cultural value. This is the reason why a book with this theme is not only necessary but also would help my colleagues to understand these times. The main thesis of this work is that we live in a stage of economic production where death is one of the main criteria of consumption. We consume death everywhere—in TV programs, novels and in reality—in order to enhance our ego. The leisure practices of our grandparents have changed to our present, more sophisticated ways that include visits to sites of disasters, mass death or human suffering such as Auschwitz, jails, disaster-spots and so forth. Of course, this obsession for death is multilayered and has many underlying factors to take into consideration. Although some studies emphasize thana-consumption as a way to understand death by means of Others' experiences, we held the opposite definition. Thana-capitalism is organized to show Others' suffering, which leads to reinforce a sentiment of narcissism, as a social status. In a society where faith in God has gone forever, not surprisingly life is seen as a great race, dotted with many participants who struggle with others to survive. In this climate, the Others' death symbolizes the opportunity to in competence.

There is no clearer metaphor evincing how thana-capitalism approaches, than the criticism over Mother Teresa and Francis. Let's remind readers that Mother Teresa will be canonized on September 4, 2016, by Pope Francis. Likely the criticism against Mother Teresa reflects how charity and piety evolved in thana-capitalism. Polemically, journalist Christopher Hitchens exalted that Mother Teresa was not a friend of ours as the media portrayed, but she was a monster whose unlimited sadism led her to minister to people with disease to be closer to God. This "missionary position" as a death-seeker looks to human suffering to enhance the self (Hitchens, 2012). Indeed, as Hitchens denounced, we live in a world where some religious leaders do not want to combat poverty in fact, but they need misery to gain further legitimacy. The missionary stance of some leaders seems to be closer to a cynic paternalism that exploits suffering as a commodity to position themselves as an unconditional source of consultation and guidance. Their original interests lie not in the eradication of poverty, war or suffering, but in their persistence. Another example of how sadism has expanded to social ethos is the recent news of Dutch tourists who throw coins to a homeless woman in Roma. In this disgusting event, viewers may see how intolerant soccer fans, who were drinking in Plaza Mayor, situated in Madrid, Spain, threw money to beggars, cheering them on to fight to pick up the coins. This event was recorded in a video, which ignited a deep discussion on the website (http://www.huffingtonpost.es/2016/03/15/aficionados-holandeses-mendigas_n_9470320.html; March 17, 2016). These sad spectacles not only entertained more than hundreds of PSV Eindhoven fans, but also the institutions did not release any communication repudiating the act. Well, the fact is that instead of cooperating with the Other or taking active participation in politics, lay-citizens in thana-capitalism adopt a naïve position—a passive attitude where witnessing replaces other reactions. Undoubtedly, the age of revolution withered away. To put this in other terms, we passed from a society that prioritized the collective protection, to a new stage where others' pain is used as an instrument of self-gratification. The concept of risk as the main value of modern capitalism as it was imagined by Beck sets the pace to death.

As discussed, death-seeker, the new class originated in thana-capitalism, encompasses similarly framed indicators. Though originally interested by heritage, they obtain naïve knowledge of the past, without any real compromise by the "Others," as charitable organizations show. Death-seekers are visually attracted by suffering, as long as watching it does not comprise further commitment to the poor. Unlike those persons who are involved in real battle against poverty such as social workers, death-seekers use the Others to reinforce their own sense of superiority. Captivated by what is transmitted in the media, they select the networks according to their individual needs, framing relations according to their desires. Educated to be winners, death-seekers feel special or exceptional in many angles and think that life is the place to show their skills. Since their gratification rests on the fact that they are the only ones chosen by God to shed light on how life should be lived, they do not hesitate to struggle against what is labeled as evil.

*Death-seekers*, as this emergent class was baptized in this book, corresponds with a new group more prone to consume death, in many cases through visual and virtual high-technology. To decipher their psychological profile into relevant points, the following scheme may help:

- They are prone to discuss events that do not involve them directly, such as the war in Middle East, or the news in *60 Minutes*. However, on rare occasions this crystalizes into real help for others.
- Starting from the premise that the present time always is better than past, they have developed an ethnocentric view of non-Western societies and ancient civilization.
- Death-seekers embrace heritage only to understand this time as the best of all possible realms.
- This group appears to claim how bad the world is only to highlight their well-ness or their particular situation. News on crimes, disasters, and sad events are used as a pretext to tell others how happy they are.
- In this case, death-seekers do not understand reality except as events that reinforce their cognitive background or previous beliefs.
- They behave in an instrumental way, using people as a means for achieving their goals. No genuine commitment to others is found.
- They have serious problems in understanding "otherness."
- Sites of mass death, disaster or suffering (thana-tourism) are often selected as the primary destinations for visiting on holidays.
- Since they are special, death consumers feel they have the right to interact with others who are well skilled, like them.
- Death-seekers support social Darwinism, where the survival of strongest is the main cultural value.
- Consuming others' suffering, they feel special, superior or more important.
- They do not take part in charitable organizations or political militancy, unless by what they visually consume through TV.
- Although they boast how altruistic they are, they follow individual and instrumental ends in their life. This opens the doors to dissociation between what they say and what they really do.
- They give excessive endorsement to democracy, which became Western civilization, as a superior ladder in the process of evolution.
- Psychologically they feel problems can be solved only through speaking. They are not pragmatists. Narcissism is enrooted in the psychological trait of death-seekers.
- They are frightful personalities that think the world is a dangerous place.

- Death-seekers are entertained by witnessing how others struggle. Very open to mythical conflagrations such as good versus evil, they symbolically associate death with condemnation: For them, the correct persons should not die.
- They have pathological problems in understanding death.
- Regardless of their political affiliation, they embrace "counterfeit politics," or the theories of conspiracy.

As a backdrop, in the first chapter I explore the concept of "dark tourism" as it was coined and studied by Sharpley and Stone. Though their concept of "thanaptosis" rests on polemic foundations, no less true is that their advances fit to my argument. In Chapter 2, entitled "Capitalism and Human Suffering," I place the problem of poverty and development under the lens of scrutiny. At a closer look, slumming or visits to slums seems to be far from dark tourist practices, but it shares the same conditions: the quest for others' pain. As death-seekers, a metaphor utilized to denote dark tourists, gazers of slums manifest their intention to be in direct contact with people to understand and redirect their own lives. However, beyond this altruist utterance remains a sadist drive. Visitors in these hot-spots develop an aura of supremacy over others who had not shared the same luck. As a result of this, suffering is understood as a commodity to enlarge the gap between the haves and have-nots. Rather, Chapter 3 is fully reserved to the analysis of the Japanese earthquake in April 2011 as well as the day the world has waited for with bated breath: the day of the Fukujima nuclear meltdown. In other distant geographies such as Argentina, many Japanese or Japanese descendants organized a cultural trip to support not only their culture but also their brothers. This opens the question of to what extent disasters call for solidarity, or for a spectacle of disasters, as it is widely discussed by Jean Baudrillard. The Fukujima case not only paves the ways for validating Baudrillard's concerns, but also offers an interesting case to expand our current understanding of the role played by cultural entertainment in disaster contexts. The fourth chapter is organized to contrast the contributions of modern sociology with our current needs to understand a new stage of capitalist production. At some extent, the society of risk sets the path to thana-capitalism, where protection no longer seems to be a requested commodity. Instead, people are in quest of consuming disasters and spectacles where others die. In fact, this obsession is based on the Western inability to accept death, which was forged by Christianity and the myth of the devil. The root of evilness, embodied in Lucifer, not only exhibits a much deeper fear of the death of sons, but also evinces the complex intersection of evilness and fertility. In contexts of famine, economic crises, or instability, the figure of the devil plays a vital role sublimating (as a scapegoat) individual responsibilities. Along the same line, the sixth chapter addresses the problem of evilness in Christianity as a neglect of pleasure, which is conducive to the protection of the elite's interests. In so doing, we place a book by Slavoj Žižek, *The Puppet and the Dwarf* (2003), under the lens of scrutiny. The problem of Christianity is not based on the impossibility to respect the law, as Žižek precludes, but on the fact that the death of Christ opens the doors to divide the world in two: victims (who as Christ sacrificed everything and himself for giving all to unknown others) and witnesses (who, insensitive to others' suffering, pursue only their own egoism). While the former are the commodities of thana-capitalism, which gives survivors a reason to live, the latter developed a discourse of supremacy to remind us that death is reserved only for weak persons. This is exactly what emulates the cinema of works such as *The Walking Dead* or any apocalyptic landscape. The spectacle of Christ's tribulation not only reminds humankind of the challenge to defy empire, but also that happiness (or eternal life—as the metaphor of survival detailed in Chapters 2 and 3) can be reached only by means of pain. This raises a more pungent question: To what extent does thana-capitalism need biocapitalism to exist? In fact, a closer look reveals how efforts of the West are devoted to expanding life, not death. In this last section, we explore the dichotomy of life, as well as biotechnology situated to protect the DNA of animals and plants in view of commercial copyright purposes and not as evidence—we embrace life, but as a sign of pathological individualism. While Nazism inaugurated the biopolitics machine, it was not ended after WWII; it was continued by the United States. The figure of Hitler as the demon of this world sets the path to superheroes such as Superman or Batman, who symbolize the ideological triumph of Darwinism on both sides of the Atlantic. What is important to discuss is the intersection of Nazism's ideology with capitalism. This sixth chapter explains how for puritans, a religious wave of self-control and indulgence became a cult of narcissism that finally led to the rise of death-seekers. Last but not least, Chapter 7 dissects the discourse of biocapitalism, following the perspective of Kaushik Sunder Rajan, who envisaged the monopolization of genomics by the "medical gaze" to impose an all-encompassing culture of the ever-consuming patient. Oriented to the needs of prevention, the constitution of postgenomic life is based on producing knowledge to reinforce the supremacy of the Anglo race, which means the hegemony of English-speaking nations over the rest of the world. This belief poses the dilemma left by Steven Pinker in a dream world where violence can be reduced by the action of enlightenment, liberality as it was formulated in England, and democracy. This section situates Pinker's argument under the critical lens of scrutiny. Paradoxically, violence was curbed to lower rates, while the world has become more unjust.

Many persons made this book possible: my wife Maria Rosa, my sons Ciro and Benjamin, and of course my wayward but not for that less lovely daughter Olivia. In addition, I am grateful for the opportunity to discuss online with remote friends such as Rodanthi Tzanelli (University of Leeds, UK), Geoff Skoll (SUNY at Buffalo, US) and Freddy Timmermann (University Silva Henriquez, Chile), who from different angles helped me to shape the idea I am exhibiting in this book. Chapters have been organized to be read separately, though they all share the same argument.

# 1 New Trends in Leisure Practices

## Introduction

Dark tourism is a phenomenon widely studied over the last decades. More substantial research has been advanced as fieldwork in dark tourism sites (Korstanje, 2011a; Korstanje & Ivanov, 2012; Seaton, 1996; Sharpley, 2005; Stone, 2012). However, such studies focused on methodologies that use tourists as the analysis's starting point. Sometimes, interviewees do not respond with honesty, or simply are not familiar with the basis of their own behavior. In Latin America people in some regions with histories of mass death are reluctant to accept tourism as their main profitable resource. Some destinations exploit death as the site's primary attraction, whereas other ones develop a negative attitude toward tourists. A more helpful way to advance this discussion, as relevant literature suggests, is that dark tourism is defined by the presence of "thanaptosis": the possibility to understand one's own (future) end through the death of others. This allows us to think of dark tourism as a subtype of heritage, even connect it to pilgrimage (Poria, 2007; Seaton, 1996; Cohen, 2011). Yet, even these studies ignore the real roots of the debate on thanatopsis and its significance for configuring the geography of dark sites. The concept of thanatopsis, which was misunderstood by some tourism scholars, such as Seaton or Sharpley, was originally coined by the American poet William Cullen Bryant (1817) to refer to the anticipation of one's own death through the eyes of others. Those who have read Bryant's poem, "Thanatopsis", will agree that the death of other people makes us feel better because we avoided temporarily our own end. We both want to retain life and are suffering because death is inevitable. To overcome this existential obstacle, we have to listen to "nature." Our death is a vital process in the transformation of the life cycle on earth. To be more precise, Bryant alludes to "thanaptosis" as the recognition that life is the primary source of happiness, which is possible only by accepting our own death. Yet, curiosity or meditation over other people's death was not present in Bryant's viewpoint—something that begs some more questions. We may ask for example: What is the connection of dark tourism and late capitalism in the First World? Is dark tourism a practice commonly accepted in "third world" cultures? What are the commonalities and differences between pilgrimage and dark tourism? Lastly, do "first world" and "third world" conceptual gaps point to the generation of links between "dark" entertainment and racism? In this conceptual discussion, one of the primary aspects to take into consideration is the role played by death in our modern world. Thanatology has shed light on human interpretation and acceptance of death. Sociologically speaking, religion and religiosity are mechanisms that alleviate human beings from the trauma of their inevitable death—mechanisms that are absent from secular societies, in which there is no expectation of afterlife (Bardis, 1981). Death is neglected by the social imaginary of industrial societies, in which life is valorized to pathological levels. Phillipe Ariès (1975) contended that secularization has expanded the boundaries of the life expectancy but paradoxically uncovered the wilderness of death. In middle times, death was something that happened to others; its exotic qualities allowed people to accept it. Death's nature was disciplined in modern societies with the help of religion, arts, science and social institutions dealing with it. Today mortality rates have diminished but death terrifies society more than ever. In his early work Phillip Stone explored why death has become a criterion of attractiveness. He argues that dark tourism has gradations ranging from darkest to lightest expressions of death. While the former are characterized by devotion to sites of extreme suffering, such as genocide, mass murders or disasters, the latter concern spaces of cultural entertainment, such as Dracula museums. Stone explains that darker and lighter products are differentiated according to the degree of suffering they offer to sightseers. Dark tourism may be defined as a sort of pilgrimage or experience of looking at sites of suffering, but what seems to be important is the function of sightseeing as an attempt to contemplate the death of the self (Stone, 2012). The visitors are not sadists enjoying the suffering of others; they experience only the possibility of death through that of the Other. This instills a message to society and allows us to learn a lesson from a tragedy, a trauma ever rememorized by survivors in visited sites of suffering. The fascination with death corresponds to a quest for new experiences that leads visitors to strengthen their social bonding with the suffering community (Stone & Sharpley, 2008). Nonetheless, a closer look suggests another interpretation. First and foremost, historians have not found any archaeological or historical evidence of dark tourism sites in medieval times or earlier. This means that tourist visits to sites of death and suffering are a new phenomenon. May dark tourism be comparable in terms of medieval pilgrims?

We must also explain why some travelers engaged in pilgrimage in cemeteries and consider the possibility that their goals and psychological motivations have nothing to do with dark tourism. Toward the consensus of a shared theory of this issue, it is often assumed that dark tourism sites exhibit spaces of great pain. To what extent these spaces are conducive to a spectacle of horror, as some sociologists put it, is one of the themes that remain unresolved. Analysts of dark tourism have criticized the fact that suffering is commercialized (Baudrillard, 1996; Foley & Lennon, 1996; Strange & Kempa, 2003;). Recent investigation has posed the question on the economic nature of death-seekers. In late modernity, postindustrial societies, far from correcting the problems that led to disaster, recycle obliterated spaces to introduce new business by facilitating the building of infrastructure for tourist income. Affected families are not economically assisted and are pressed to move away, to live to the peripheries of the city. Death and mass suffering seem to be employed to reinforce the pillars of capitalism. At this stage, tourism seems to be conducive to a logic of exploitation in which death is the primary resource of attractiveness. Particularly, this makes tourism a resilient industry (Klein, 2007; Korstanje, 2011c; Korstanje & Clayton, 2012; Korstanje & Tarlow, 2012; Verma & Jain, 2013). Some scholars have explained that dark tourism is praised as a pedagogical pursuit, giving a message to survivors of tragedies. This message is subject to the degree of authenticity the site can generate (Cohen, 2011). One wonders whether dark tourism has evolved now with the help of business mobility to a new resiliency mechanism—a way to face trauma. In an early study, Maximiliano Korstanje and Stanislav Ivanov (2012) delineated a strong connection between dark tourism and psychological resilience, arguing that the former was developed by a community to overcome adversities. Disaster and historical trauma teach a lesson to survivors and their community, thus restructuring it politically. The function of dark tourism consists in situating death within the human understanding of past, present and future. Death generates substantial changes in the life of survivors. A community that faced disasters or experienced extreme pain runs a serious risk of disintegration, if a profound sentiment of pride for its adversities is not developed: otherwise put, to reassert unity, its society tries to find ways to narrativize (explain) the disaster. Dark tourism is conducive to that, but under certain circumstances as practice it may instigate chauvinism and ethnical superiority that may lead to racist and ethnocentric tendencies. This happens simply because the feeling of superiority helps survivors to balance the frustrations and the sentiment of losses in a post-disaster context. Survivors feel that after all, not everything is lost. Gods gave them another opportunity because of their moral strengths. If this sentiment of exceptionality is not duly regulated, survivors develop pathological attachments to suffering, by blurring pain with pleasure. White and Frew (2013) suggested that dark tourism sites are politically designed to express a message to the community historically, politically and emotionally connected to them. Victims and their families proffer a variety of interpretations of such messages and the very social trauma that they experienced. There are no clear boundaries or indicators to mark a unified site of memory; heritage is shaped by political interests and sometimes centralized national discourse around dark sites is not accepted by the community in unison. Sather-Wagstaff (2011) presents an original thesis based on her auto-ethnography in Ground Zero in New York. She argues that dark tourism sites incite sentiments of loss and mourning, but the very definition of loss is at large. Dark tourism shrines such as that of Ground Zero are reminders of the paining event, given that death is not only irreversible, but also inevitable. Visitors are invited to feel what victims felt—even though these emotions are inauthentic. From the Hiroshima disaster to the collapse of the World Trade Center, Sather-Wagstaff argues that disasters should tell a story that helps control the trauma or sense of loss. The solidarity offered to the United States after the terrorist attack in New York City was a clear example of how people are united in contexts of uncertainty. Death's function is to strengthen the social bond. By introducing human suffering, dark tourism breaks the influence of ideology.

As carrier of ideology, heritage imposes a one-sided argument created externally to enable consumers to accept governmental policies they would otherwise reject. Where heritage is politically rooted, pain induces disinterested empathy. Death wakes up the society from its slumber, creating the conditions to adopt substantial changes. Emotions transcend national boundaries, questioning the ethnocentrism of heritage. One wonders if dark tourism is a continuation of medieval pilgrimage, which was based on unmediated experiential connection to the visited (sacred) site. Even though in medieval times death was present in almost all institutions and representations of daily life, medieval pilgrims should not be equated with contemporary dark tourists. Unlike modern sightseers, medieval travelers would visit sacred sites so as to redeem their sins, ask for forgiveness or supplicate saints to negotiate with God a solution to their pains or big troubles. Although venerated, for medieval travelers death was not a problem but the beginning of a new, better life. In this respect, contemporary dark tourism exhibits the opposite dynamic. "Secular tourists" are not interested in the life of others, nor in their heritage or biography. They want to avoid their own death. The present thesis contends that tourists exorcise death by ritualizing the death of others so as to symbolically expand their own life expectancy (Tzanelli, 2014; 2015b). Michel Foucault's conception of biopolitics can be mobilized to explain how this works: using Nazism, Foucault argues that biopolitics is derived from the concept of "bio-power," which plays a pervasive role, because on one hand it expands life but on the other it imposes mass death. Nazis improved their technique of biotechnology by manipulating the life of others—dubbed under-humans or *Unter-mensch*. Divested of their rights, some ethnicities and minorities were subjected to the Nazi's systematic bureaucratization of death (Foucault, 1969; 2007; Lemke, 2001).

In some respect, the genocide perpetrated by Nazis in Europe against civilian targets not only ignited a hot discussion respecting to the intersection of death and life, but also transcended any ethical ontology of the subject. Nazis has advanced much in bio-technology, cloning cells and other experiments associated to make a better life in earth, but paradoxically, at the same time it was achieved thanks to a radical extermination of global population. Their desires were intended to forge a superior race, whose destiny was marked by governing inferior others even with the possibility of enslaving them to construct an empire that would take 1,000 years to build. Of course, although this insane project never was success, the main core of this ideology was passed to the United States (in a sublimated form). The archetype of superman not only emulates all Nazis hopes but also reinforces the narcissist climate of social Darwinism that facilitated the advance of Hitler to power. Žižek says that Christianity nourishes a discourse of betrayal, since Christ was betrayed to become in God, but things seem to be more profound. Christianity was erected under the figure of death as its main value. As anthropologist, when I was doing my fieldwork in Amazonia, natives told me that they wanted to know further on a religion where the main god is tortured and sacrificed. Evidently, the signs of Christ in the crucifixion offers a sadist spectacle incomparable in other mythologies. Though we are accustomed, the image of a person exposed and savagely hanging from a crucifix sounds really disgusting for everyone who does not share our faith.

This is exactly the metaphor of thana-capitalism, and how death worked as a cultural entertainment. Nazis not only completed the tribulation of Christ, but they cynically wanted to expand to the rest of unworthy humankind. In fact, the end of WWII resulted in the collapse of Nazism, but its ideology persisted in indirect, insidious ways. The ideal of the "superhuman"—the man of outstanding powers destined to deter corruption and evilness—persisted alongside the scientific fascination with eugenics, cloning and bio-technology. As Jeremy Rifkin put it, "the coming age of commerce" resulted from the Nazi's ideology of a selected race. This ideology, introduced by British eugenics, never died in the United States (Rifkin, 1998). In a world where people are commoditized as bio-resources to laboratories to prolong the life of elites, death is expended to peripheral world zones. As Naomi Klein explains, capitalism allows for the recycling of affected communities in post-disaster areas into new forms of consumption. The experience of shock is used by governments on their citizens to make them accept policies they would otherwise reject (Klein, 2007). Of course, this argument connects to David Harvey's (1989) discussion of "creative destruction": capitalism persists by destroying social landscapes and institutions only to be reconstructed following other ends. Some philosophical concerns arise around the role played by technology in this process. As Richard Hofstadter puts it, not only did capitalism make use of profits, exploiting the workforce, but also introduced successfully "social Darwinism," which reinforced the axiom of the survival of fittest as a new ethics. In other words, we "play the game" because the opportunities to defeat our opponents are exaggerated (Hofstadter, 1963). The competition fostered by the ideology of capitalism offers the salvation for few ones, at the expense of the rest. To realize the dream of joining the "selected people," we accept the rules. Whenever one of our direct competitors fails, we feel an insane happiness. I argue that a similar mechanism is activated during our visit to dark tourism sites: we do not strive to understand, we are just happy because we escaped death and have more chances to win the game of life. This argument is examined in the next section. George Mead, one of the fathers of symbolic interactionism, questioned why paradoxically many people show preference to unpleasant and bad stories in the news and the press. What is our fascination with other peoples' suffering? He assertively concludes that the self is configured through its interaction with others. This social dialectic introduces anticipation and interpretation as the two pillars of the communicative process. The self feels happiness through the other's suffering—a rite necessary to avoid or think 8 about one's own potential pain. Starting from the premise that the self is morally obliged to assist the other to reinforce a sentiment of superiority, avoidance preserves the ethical base of social relationships (Mead, 2009). Mead's reflections could be applied to the act of visiting dark tourism shrines. To understand this, we can revert to the myth of Noah and its pivotal role in the salvation of the world in Christianity. The legend tells us that God, annoyed by the corruption of human beings, mandated to Noah to construct an ark. Noah's divine mission consisted of gathering and adding a pair per species to his ark so as to achieve the preservation of natural life. The world was destroyed by the great flood, but life diversity survived. At first glance, the myth's moral message is based on the importance of nature and the problem of sin and corruption. But when examined more carefully, the myth poses the dilemma of competition: at any "tournament" or game, there can be only one winner. In the archetypical Christian myth, Noah and the selected species stand as the only witnesses of everything and everyone else's death. I argue that the curiosity and fascination for death comes from this founding myth, which is replicated in plays to date, stating that only one can be crowned the winner. Even, the television show *Big Brother*, which was widely studied by sociologists and researchers of visual technology, rests on this principle. Only a selected few live forever on the screen, as is the case in religious myths such as those of Protestantism and Catholicism (both based on doctrines of salvation and understandings of death). In fact, Stone explains that sensual experience is determined by a similar premise: a reminder that we, the survivors, are in the race and our sole purpose is to finish our journey. Brilliantly, Bauman reminds us in his books *Consuming Life* and *Liquid Fear* that life has no meaning without death. For him, the capitalist ethos has changed the mentality of citizens, who do not even fulfil the function of production automata any longer. As commodities, workers are today exploited to sustain the principle of massive consumption, which is encouraged by capitalism. The show *Big Brother* is such an example of how people enter competitions as commodities, to be selected and bought by others. Participants in this reality show know that only one will win, and the rest will "die." *Big Brother*, for Bauman, emulates life in capitalist societies; it does so by enhancing the lifestyle of the few by "producing" pauperization for the rest. The modern state keeps in pace with the liberal market to monopolize people's sense of security. This does not mean that states are unable to keep security, but that the market is controlling consumption by the imposition of fear. If human disasters such as Hurricane Katrina, in which thousands of poor citizens were left to die, show the pervasive nature of capitalism, the "show of disaster" releases it from the responsibilities of the event. The sense of catastrophe, like death, serves to cover the inhuman nature of capitalism (Bauman, 2007; 2008). This spectacularized society has only one answer to crisis, when its economic system is at risk. The real causes of the disaster are ignored thanks to the spectacle of death, which is reproduced in the media and famous TV series. What do we really know about the real causes of Auschwitz or 9/11? Could a museum explain the complexity of human nature? Bauman would say it would not. Any attempt to sacralize dying as a spectacle is the prelude of its neglect. Dark tourism is not different from spectacles such as those of the FIFA World Cup and reality shows such as *Big Brother*. All of them proclaim ideologically that only one may be crowned winner (Korstanje, Tzanelli & Clayton, 2014).

## Conclusion

Dark tourism is characterized by a strange fascination or at least curiosity for what specialists call "death spaces." The term refers to sites where the death of others is commoditized as a tourist product. For that, Tony Johnston argues that dark tourism research adopts three different models or modular ways of analysis: the first involves "building conceptual models" to explain how death is configured the by social imaginary; the second, prioritizes empirical supply of information about the characteristics of sites and destination demands; and lastly, it attempts with the help of the "tourist experience" to explore the psychological drives of visitors as well as the structuration of their experience (Johnston, 2013). Though "thana-tourism" or "dark tourism" has gained attention in tourism-led scholarship around the world, its study's symbolic epicentre still remains England. The rich archaeological legacy and fascination of ancient Anglo-culture for death may prove key factors in constructing a widely accepted paradigm. Nonetheless, two major discourses within current research on dark tourism are flawed: on one hand, analysts claim that Catholicism induced a curiosity for death that resulted in medieval pilgrimages to saints' tombs and shrines. They claim that these types of sacred travels resulted in the orientation of the modern tourist to the consumption of things that have to do with death. Secondly, dark tourism sites are represented as spaces of heritage and pilgrimage which are intensified by the landscape of death. The movement of the tourist to these sites is motivated by their encounter with death. In this thesis dark tourism serves as a mediator between the visitor's future death, the appreciation of their life via the death of others (Stone, 2005; Stone & Sharpley, 2008). The present essay explored not only the anthropological roots of dark tourism but also the influence of late capitalism in shaping the allegory of death. In stark opposition to the medieval traveler, dark tourist consumers seek to reinforce their life via another's death. In contrast to what the specialized literature suggests, dark tourism reinforces the modern egocentrism to enjoy "the brother's tragedy." By replicating the myth of Noah's ark, capitalism introduced in people's lives the necessity of competition as prerequisite for their inclusion in the "league" of the selected few. Life then assumes the function of a great race in which only one can be the winner and the rest will lose. If tragedy confers to survivors the aura of exemplary civilization, it comes at great cost. Happiness for the other's death is a sign we still remain in contention for the final fight. From *Big Brother* to *The Hunger Games*, the salvation of one by the ruin of the whole has fed into an all-consuming ideology of our modern world. As such, the ethics of dark tourism emulates a new economic form of exploitation that characterizes the capitalism.

# 2   Capitalism and Human Suffering

## Introduction

With the advent of twenty-first century, a great variety of risks and dangers place tourism industry in jeopardy. From terrorism to virus outbreaks, policy makers face a great challenge in order for maintaining the competitiveness of their destinations. This is the reasons why security recently turned in the bulwark of marketing and tourism management (Tarlow, 2014). In parallel it is safe to say that new segments tourists defy the classic "Sun and Beach" product. The question whether the old concept of beauty has been replaced by the adrenaline of new experiences, is one of the main topics to be deciphered throughout this essay review. Tourists not only are seeking new sensations, but also they even place their lives at risk to obtain authentic experiences. New trends such as war tourism, dark tourism or even doom tourism seem to be on the agenda of governments and marketing experts. Are modern consumers attracted by violence? Or are capitalism and poverty interlinked?

As this question has been formulated, some voices have appeared in last years, highlighting the benefits of slum-tourism in pacifying ghettos or hot-spots where crime, violence and other pathologies coexist. States should contribute to expand these practices not only to improve the quality life of slum-dwellers, but also to disarticulate crime and cartels of drugs. The present chapter discusses to what an extent not only slum-touring is a fertile ground to revitalize the economies of relegated ethnicities, but also the pervasive role of tourists in gazing "dangerous Others." Derivative questions delineated the argument through this section, such as, Is poverty a commodity to be replicated by this new trend? Or can natives live better by adopting programs of slum-tourism? The discussion on the conceptual framework on this matter remains fuzzy and unclear. The first sections of the chapter delve into the problem of poverty and the different treatment for economic waves. Finally, the concept of slum-tourism is placed under the lens of scrutiny to present alternative viewpoints to expand the current understanding of this slippery matter. Typically, visitors of slums areas once they are interviewed manifest their needs of taking distance of enclave tourism interacting with natives. Whereas for some scholars, it exhibits a sadist obsession for enjoying "the Other's pain," others think "this is a valid way" of learning a message that serves for their own lives. Here a point of entry in this discussion arises: *What is the true message of slum-tourism?*

## Why Does Poverty Exist?

Liberal economists Acemoglu and Robinson argue polemically that poverty exists not as a result of eagerness stimulated by capitalism, but by the "extractive institutions of Third World," that balks competition among stakeholders and institutions. In their best-selling book *Why Nations Fail?*, these experts say that two countries (or cities) formed by the same ethnicity, demography and topography may reach diverse levels of development, wealth, education and health. Responding why this happens is the primary attempt of the project. When political power is concentrated in few hands, the wealth is not distributed to the rest of society, creating poverty and backwardness. In view of this, nondemocratic societies are prone to perpetuate narrowly formed elites, since governments are not removed by elections. And of course, its main thesis is aimed at denouncing that democracy (in the United States and Europe) not only in how governments address the claims of their respective citizens, but also in cultural issues:

> "Why are the institutions of United States more conducive to economic success than those of Mexico or, for that matter, the rest of Latin America? The answer to this question lies in the way the different societies formed during the early colonial period. An institutional divergence took place then, with implications lasting into the present day. To understand this divergence, we must begin right at the foundation of the colonies in North and Latin America." (Acemoglu & Robinson, 2012, p. 9)

Spanish settled, hosting the indigenous leaders, and once done, their attempts were aimed at creating new elite, which obliges the native to pay taxes and other tributes. The conquest in Americas was based on the idea that others should work for the Crown. Elegantly, this founding event marked forever the destiny of Latin America. Unlike, Anglo-world, Latin American elites organized the exploitation of their peoples in view of the monopoly of wealth, they expect to be returned. The British Empire, when its colonists arrived in the Americas, discovered that not only was it not possibile to find gold and other precious metals, which were in areas already occupied by Spaniards, but also it was pressed to survive with its own arms. Labor and trade with others here played a vital role by configuring the political system of North America. The culture of exploitation was unknown, authors add, for the United States and Canada, and therefore it was the reason behind the rapid adoption of democracy as the first form of governance. While the Latin American region had a high density of population that facilitated exploitation by Iberian empires, in North America the Crown had serious problems to incorporate the same institutions used by Spain and Portugal. This generated a system of incentive where hard work and egalitarian rights paved the pathways to the formation of democracy. Among its strengths, the book addresses historic processes in a coherent and clear way, doing the best to understand the formation and evolution of poverty. Basically, it starts from the premise two "twin nations" may develop contrasting economies to date. Political institutions explain us how what now are striking differences; they were not existed in ancient times. As an example, a South Korean case is asserted as a proof the theory is correct.

> "The People of South Korea have living standards similar to those of Portugal and Spain. To the north, in the so called Democratic People's Republic of Korea, or North Korea, living standards are akin to those of a sub-Saharan African country, about one-tenth of the average living standard in South Korea. The health of North Koreans is in an even worse state; the average North Korean can expect to live ten years less than their cousins of the 38th parallel." (Acemoglu & Robinson, 2012, p. 71)

While North Korea adopted a communist authoritarian government that central-ized the wealth in a small minority (elite); South Koreans experienced a substan-tial change in their institutions that helped for democracy to be enthralled in the country. The entire book centers on a historical approach that attempts to unravel the puzzle of wealth. In the second chapter authors explore how poor countries are in such situation not by reason of their cultures or geographies, but rather by their governments. The way politics induce society to follow certain incen-tives, while others are discarded, explains how prosperity and poverty surface. Competition among social institutions and bank system cemented the possibility to foster stronger networks that accelerated the growth in the democratic societies. It is not surprising that

> "The reason that the United States has a banking industry that was radi-cally better for the economic prosperity of the country has nothing to do with differences in the motivation of those who owned the banks. Indeed, the profit motive, which underpinned the monopolistic nature of the banking industry in Mexico, was present in United States too. But this profit motive was channeled differently because of the radically different US institutions." (Acemoglu & Robinson, 2012, p. 5)

Those nations that fail today are determined by a "logic of exploitation" escaping to "absolutism." This atmosphere of nonparticipation for ordinary peoples engen-ders dictatorial institutions, which are not prepared to manage successfully the economy. Acemoglu and Robinson argue convincingly that prosperity and wealth must not be engineered or designed by means of rational policies introduced by experts, whenever the culture is mined by authoritarian basis. They are the results from deliberative democracies worldwide. This begs the question of how a society passes from restrictive to adopt participative institutions.

Though eloquent, Acemoglu and Robinson's argument is flawed by ethnocentrism. It validates an error of interpretation, by which the explanation of behaviors is inferred by characteristics of the groups where individuals belong. This means that democracy and prosperity are social construes only valid in capitalist societies; they are not universal goods by themselves. Therefore, the correlation between both is given in this one-sided direction, where there is not serious discussion of how democracy has evolved, neither its diverse meanings in the threshold of time. There are many other nations which are free to choose to live in another way. Paradoxically, envisaging democracy as a universal value is a betrayal to the self-determination of others (the center of democracy).

To put this in bluntly, if we think values such as prosperity, longer life-spans, voting, health and expectation of life are good for peoples, in esse, we must assume the rest of cultures should accept them. However, other non-Western cultures may see in the Occident serious pathologies accelerated by Anglo democracy, such as "insomnia," "distress," "suicides," "crime," "competence and job insecurity "sexual abuses," "drug abuses" and so forth. This book ignores precisely what anthropology showed one century ago; this means that the economic factor resulted from the introduction of rationality as a new way of relations, which suggest Europe and its spirit was resulted from evolution of superior "values" over others of "weaker character." The discourse of rationality, embodied in the theory of development, not only indebted the world, but also posed the world in one of its more radical crisis (R. Rajan, 2010; Stiglitz, 2003). Defining the nation's success, which depends on the degree of wealth, or per capita income, as this book did, corresponds with an "ethnocentric" mechanism of discipline aimed at creating a need in non-Western societies, oddly the needs of being a developed and modern nation. Last but not least, the concatenated failures to expand development beyond West, never opened the discussion around the responsibility of international banks or financial organizations such as IMF or World Bank, analysts and academicians delve into cultural pathologies, enrooted in third-world countries as civil wars, corruption, ethnic cleansing and so forth (Esteva & Prakash, 1998). To our end, philosophically speaking this was the big problem of Europe to understand the "otherness," the "difference" was conceptualized as a glitch to fix instead of a fundamental character of other collective beings.

Doubtless, capitalism represented an economic revolution resulted from a combination of factors, but three were determinants, the discovery and conquest of the Americas, which prompted a trade expansion, together the technological breakthroughs as well as a planned production that altered the conception of labor. From the inception of economy as an academic discipline, poverty was an eternal concern for diverse scholars. Paradoxically, the production or wealth of capital-owners equated to the limited opportunities for workforce (Heilbroner, 1995)—in terms of Lester Thurow (2001), a type of zero-sum society. In capitalized economies, any change in one direction produces counter-effects in other sectors which should be planned and corrected. However, the oil crisis in 70s decade objected the omnipotence of West by reminding the importance of energetic resources to keep a scale system of production and the problems they were no longer affordable. This suggests that the growth of GDP sometimes is not determined by a radical improvement of poor people's living conditions or housing. As David Harvey (1989) puts it, postmodernism was a project originally created to replace Fordism that characterized America over decades. From that moment on, thinking economy in long terms was a utopia simply because the means of production changed to new decentralized forms. The oil's embargo posed by Arab countries generated to collateral damages for Western economies; the rise of poverty and the end of labor. In this respective, worker unions not only weakened their capacity to negotiate with capital owners, but the social trust was undermined. As Taylor-Gooby (2004) clarifies, the welfare state has serious problems in its attempts to protect the whole portion of citizens because of two main reasons: The adoption of new technologies to enhance the already system of production buttressed profits but reduced notably the number of arms necessary for working. The concept of efficiency as it was formulated by economists plays a crucial role by legitimizing the competition in the market as well as introducing capitalist values as the best values possible in this world. Ideologically, exegetes of capitalism believe the world as it is today was ever in the ancient past, ignoring that as a young cultural project, capitalism is not older than 300 years. In parallel, the high technology associated with the expansion of life expectancy resulted in rapid aging in the economically active population. Modern nation-states were not only subject to the dilemma by fixing further taxes over labor force, but were unable to improve the labor conditions. Therefore, the decline of welfare state sets the pace to a new concept to alleviate the negative effects of financial crashes, *the theory of develop-ment*. In other terms, though expectancy of life was extended as never before, the daily life turned in a more insecure place where uncertainness and vulnerability of working classes rose.

Within social science no consensus was reached according to the theory of development. In this respect, Phillip McMichael (2012) describes the ebbs and flows of development from the outset up to date. This global and all-encompassing view allows readers not only to understand the North-South dependency, but also the role played by "development" in such a process. In perspective, McMichael shows his erudition and familiarity with this issue. Instead of focusing on the protection of state, as it has been formulated by development theories, globalization emphasis on the "free market" as the ideological conduit of politics. The protection of interests of global powers consists not only in securing the food production (in south) to be exported to North, but also in the set of loans to keep "the market integration." The key factor of neoliberalism is "governance," which means the coordination of NGOs by accessing information and material resources to fulfill the gaps left by "failed states." Today, corporate outsourcing is at a crucial point. The market used to determine the contours of states. Failure of development to achieve a fairer distribution of wealth implies the discussion of three major themes such as the manipulation of debts (debts crisis), the use of outsourcing to relegate the authority of state, and the problems of poverty and sustainability. McMichael reconsiders what specialists dubbed "the crisis of mass-consumerism and global capital" as well as posing new lessons to reduce the increasing levels of poverty worldwide. His main thesis is that Europe, by the introduction of colonialism, established an ideological background for legitimizing their submissions to its overseas colonies. The exploitation of the non-European Others had a pervasive nature. The process of decolonization, centuries later, witnessed the rise of demands of periphery in order for central powers to allow an autonomous government. The rights of democracy become a universal claim. McMichael explains that imperial powers alluded to the theory of "development" to maintain the old colonial borders. Now violence sets the pace to financial dependency. The WWII end conjoined to Truman's administration led the United States to implement a wide range credit system to save the world from Communism. This program mushroomed into the development theory. However, this financial aid brought modification in the system of agriculture to more intensive methods wreaking havoc on the condition of farmers who were pressed to migrate to larger urban cities. Furthermore, the imposition of new borders post WWII forced many ethnicities to live with others under the hegemony of nation-state. This resulted in a lot of ethnic cleansing, conflicts and warfare that obscured the original ends of financial aid programs issued by IMF or World Bank. Undoubtedly, the inconsistencies of World Bank in administering the development-related programs not only were admitted but also it woke up some nationalist reactions in the nonaligned countries. To restore the order, a new supermarket revolution surfaced: *globalization*.

This stage, characterized by a decentralized production, undermined the barriers of nation-states globalizing investments in those countries were working condition were more convenient for financial elite. In this vein, two alarming situations were found. An increase in the unemployment and the decline of unionization in the North was accompanied with the arrival of international business corporations seduced by the low cost of workers in the South. The proliferation of slums and ghettos everywhere not only explains the failure of development-related programs, but also the inefficiency of officials to orchestrate more sustainable plans of social care.

Not surprisingly, if the persistence of mass poverty in the world was caused by modern capitalism, we will delve into how poverty was ideologically digested by Americans and how welfare sector failed to make a fairer society. It is safe to say in America there is a "culture of poverty" which has not been eradicated by the successive democratic governments. James Patterson (1994) finds in the roots of American culture a much deeper refusing for poverty which defies the archetype of puritan worker. Although structurally organized in classes, one of the main problems of poverty is the scale we use to compare some cohorts that have nothing in common. Those poor workers in 1910 in rural cities are pretty different than the urban poor in 1930, and vice versa. The moot point lies in the historical position of poverty to achieve a lack of dialogue among classes and races. While Negro (or Afro-Americans) lived in inferior conditions of whites, Latinos and Asian Americans show serious asymmetries at the time of conducting a comparative research. To what extent social warfare was a conceptual doctrine undermined by policy makers in the United States seems to be a problem very hard to grasp. Furthermore, Americans never adopted laborism as an alternative ideology to promote benefits for the work-force. The prevailing individualism conjoined to the struggle to achieve goals were two key factors that led the country to a type of meritocracy. Patterson points out that

"American Reformers were motivated by the suffering of the poor but by more functional, less altruistic reasons: achieving religious salvation, enhancing their social status, supply the cheap labor, controlling the dangerous classes. One nineteen-century reformer warned of that fermenting mass of vice and ignorance which [threatens] the safety of our social and political institutions." (Patterson, 1994, p. 31)

The poor, as an emergent element of capitalist system, were psychologically labeled as a pathology, waking up the anxiety in other productive classes, which were loathe to accept the idea of intervention to reverse its conditions. Therefore, the tactic of "blaming the victim" not only characterized the climate of different government, but also influenced notably the argument of economists. In a seminal introductory chapter, Thomas Pogge enumerates the theories that defend capitalism as a promising project which in some suitable contexts may bring equality worldwide. For Pogge, we should reconsider the problem of poverty as one of the main limitations proponents of capitalism are unable to address. In this world, some fewer central nations have much wealth while others live in miserable conditions. Since poverty has been naturalized from the discourse of exegetes of free market, as a necessary evil, it is important to discuss if extreme poverty for example in slums, represents a clear human rights violation. In fact, Pogge adheres to the thesis poverty can be resulted from intervention, which means that a superpower produces asymmetrical relations of exchange (trade) causing glitches in peripheral economies, or by omission. Whatever the case may be, the fallacy of capitalism consists in pointing out free market as the only vehicle to the eradication of poverty. Whenever this belief does not just to reality, economists adduce cultural background issues in peripheral governments. As Pogge observed,

"Over the past two decades, China has been the great success story, achieving phenomenal growth and per capita income. So China's example is now often used to argue that the rules of World economy are favorable to the poor countries and conducive to poverty eradication. These arguments, too, commit a some-all fallacy. Exporters in the poor countries compete over the same heavily protected rich country markets. Thanks to this extraordinarily ability to deliver quality product cheaply in large quantities, China has done extremely well in this competition. But this great success has had catastrophic effects in many poor countries by reducing their exporters market share and export prices." (Pogge, 2007, p. 45)

Following this argument, poverty would never result from the lack of capitalism, but also seems to be its immediate consequence. Far from being solved, the problem of poverty as well as the ever-increasing protests against professional politics evinces not only that his diagnosis is right, but also that his book gives a coherent explanation of the impossibility of globalization as a project. Methodologically, McMichael's book overemphasizes the study-case without paying heed to the conceptual background of capitalism. The configuration of "social Darwinism," that aggravated the competition among workers, as well as the role of predestination brought by reform, are not coherently analyzed by author. What is well observed by our author is that the economic asymmetries between a richer class and a created poorer underclasses is given by the ideological nature of reform. In other terms, the archetype of "uphill city" where few are saved while the whole is condemned, serves as an example replicated on earth. Capitalism monopolizes the financial power in a few hands at the time as the workforce is left to an extreme competition (survival of the strongest). As films such as *Hunger Games* and even television series such as *Big Brother* show, the salvation of few entails the ruins of the whole. Since participants are not cognizant of their low probabilities to win (in a game that has a sole winner), all-against-all competition obscures the real goals behind exploitation.

In his recently published work *Le Nouveau Luxe* (2013), French philosopher Yves Michaud explains that the world has changed after the revolution of capitalism. Citing the work of Robert Frank and Philip Cook, *The Winner-Takes-All Society*, he acknowledges that we are witnessing a society where the winner takes all in one go, leaving the rest with nothing. This applies not only in cinema where only few survive, while the rest are killed or tragically die, but in sports, business and even in real life where some few millionaires gather recalcitrant wealth. The luxury which was historically characterized as a sign of distinction for the upper classes, now has converted into "a pretext for lay people to feel outstanding." The luxury of objects which was seen in the society of our grandparents sets the pace to the luxury of experiences, a subtler and complex phenomenon where citizens pay for expensive safaris, trips to exotic destinations or even stay in luxurious hotels to exacerbate their own narcissism. All this is oriented to simulated exceptional and unique experiences which lead consumers to authenticity. This new luxury, far from disappearing, stimulates temporal experiences instead of the acquisition of objects (Michaud, 2013).

Returning to Pogge, there is a radical criticism on the theory that points out those countries with fewer probabilities for democracy show lower levels of wealth than other where democracy is already consolidated. Given these global rules as granted, financial elites held the thesis democracy flourishes only in some promising cultural backgrounds. In that way, they are irresponsible for the economic failure in hands of underdeveloped countries. While wealth in main economies is concentrated in a tighter circle, the rest of the world is facing serious problems with poverty and pauperism. Far from leading underdeveloped countries toward development, the exchange between richer and poorer countries is given in asymmetrical conditions (Pogge, 2007). A further philosophical inquiry in this direction not only is necessary but also remains unchecked. After all, as Patterson anticipated, the dilemma of poverty depends on the lens how it is perceived. One might speculate that extreme poverty not only exhibits the ethical limits of capitalism but also represents a human rights violation. While the former is unquestionable, the latter should be re-considered in view of Rawls's assertion. One of the aspects that Rawls misunderstood was the fusion between justice and institutional action. Starting from the premise that the concept of justice should be framed as a consequence of social background and institutions where the society has evolved. Putting in egalitarian conditions, two societies, for example, A and B, will develop different levels of wealth and production. Given the original possibilities of all members, any intervention of wealthier society over poorer would sound unjust. However, as Pogge observed, if wealthier states manipulate the rules of trade to gain further profits, as has happened historically, it represents a serious offence that is endorsed by the First World. In fact, whenever poverty is caused by external interests such as eagerness, or military-led invasions, it exhibits a real violation of human dignity. In this discussion, Campbell (2007) contends that Pogge was in the correct side by confirming poverty vulnerates the right of peripheral nations in the moment superior economic powers take advantage of their situation to exploit others or abusing from asymmetrical negotiations. Of course, Campbell understands, scholars should distinguish one thing consists in harming, but others are related not to intervene with financial aid. The problem does not lie in the intersection of poverty, justice and human rights where Rawls goes, but in the fact that global poverty in this World was caused by global institutions and legal rules which endorsed local governments. Given the problem in these terms, the alarming state of exclusion and poverty would be a sign of a global program posed by central nations and accepted by peripheral economies to exploit their respective citizens. This begs the following questions: Why are some countries developed while others remain under-developed? Are these difference rooted in cultural background?

Again, the process of globalization liberated the offshoring companies to conduct their investments in low-labor countries, which vulnerates the working conditions of many workers situated in peripheral zones. Therefore, Mark Hanson (2008) claims that the problems of underdeveloped economies lie in the lack of interests or skills in educating the workforce to compete with others in the marketplace. He cites the examples of South Korea, as opposed to Mexico, to convince readers that not capitalism but instead the lack of training and educated manpower to face future challenges is the problem. Since the age of ideology is over, globalization not only undermines social conflict, but also is blurring national borders in order for nations to obtain greater capacities to compete in the global market.

However, not all academicians are in consensus with this thesis. Others voices, such as Alvaro de Vita (2007), alert us to the fact that evolution of capitalism not only concentrated further wealth in few hands, but also paved the ways for the rise of exclusion, which created more poverty and misery. If we evaluate GINI coefficient from 1988 to available information in 1993, it rose from 62.8 to 66. Nonetheless, to what extent humanitarian aid reverses the situation created by colonialism first and globalization later seems to be one of the points which need further discussion. It is tempting to say, international responsibility for local problems is a way for local elite to avoid any liability for its policies. Although de Vita acknowledges, people and not institutions transcend the barriers of society to improve their living conditions, no less true is that financial institutions as they were designed, do not offer further probabilities to poor countries to resolve their lack of investment. It creates a vicious circle which is aggravated by higher tariffs imposed by central economies to the agriculture of periphery.

Discursively this scourge, some scholars ignore, operates from paradigms which cannot be violated because it involves powerful social actors. This means that the reduction of poverty is not an impossible project, unless by the fact it defies the status quo. Pragmatists did the incorrect thing in neglecting poverty as something else than a consequence of organizational interaction. If Rawls falls in a caveat it consists in believing the world is an scenario of mutual cooperation.

Following this argument, Marc Fleurbaey (2007) argues that the main limitation in Rawls's development relates to the impossibility of the poor to make decisions about conditions of flexibility and liberty. The poor are even daily constrained to accept decisions made in other circles. Secondly, given the fact that the poor have little probability of changing their style of life, they should receive help from others. If this happens, violence interpelates subject to create a cycle of dependency of the poor upon the richer classes. Although this is the moral quandary Rawls leaves open, he does not show the minimal attempt to discuss poverty as a form of oppression. The world where Rawls theorizes not only does not exist, but also is very hard to imagine. The question whether liberty and not the law, paves the ways for a distribute society, there is no reason to think richer countries nowadays should make the pertinent changes in order for the economic world to be fairer for the third world. Rawls's conception seems to be pro status quo. This discussion fits our argument in two senses. On one hand, poverty is neither a human condition nor a human right violation which merits urgent intervention; but on the other hand, poverty exists because there are institutions which are conducive to this state of exploitation. Given this situation, over recent years, it becomes in a criterion of spectacle which is offered to international tourists who visit slums and ghettos in quest of sense for their lives.

## The Voice of Liberalism

In *Bailouts or Bail-Ins?* economists Roubini and Setser alert on the problems of modern capitalism as well as the IMF intervention to rescue all economies once crisis takes hit. This opens the doorstep toward a great dilemma, if the country is left adrift a contagion effects may surface. Otherwise, there are not sufficient funds to help all countries which enter in recession. The role of IMF by expanding loans in the 1990s not only was unsustainable but also produced counter-productive effects.

> "The use of IMF loans can also cause confusion. Does IMF bail out a country or the government of that country?. The correct answer is both. The IMF helps a crisis country by lending to its government. An IMF loan often does rescue a country in trouble because its government is having difficulties in repaying its own debts. The additional reserves from an IMF loan are used to avoid the default on the government's foreign currency debt. However, an IMF rescue loan has other potential issues. IMF lending to a crisis country's central bank can finance emergency lending to support a country's baking system, which otherwise would have had a trouble paying domestic depositors or international bank credits." (Roubini & Setser, 2004)

Then, despite the help of IMF, why not only has poverty persisted, but also was duplicated over the last decades?

What are the claims of liberalism with respect to government interventions? In his book *Capitalism and Freedom*, Milton Friedman says,

> "First, the scope of government must be limited. Its major function must be to protect our freedom both from the enemies outside our gates and from our fellow-citizens: to preserve law and order, to enforce private contracts, to foster competitive markets." (Friedman, 1982, p. 2)

The centrality of government, Friedman adds, should be effaced in favor of individual rights. Then, following liberal thinking, centralized states run greater risk of developing poverty and misery than do liberal democracies. Here we have to be cautious at time of linking liberalism with democracy. Any government must avoid the effective ways of equality and welfare, or the paternalist views to intervene in the cycles of economies. Friedman starts his premise, populisms over last decades, claimed the hope of further equality to centralize their interventions. At some extent, liberalism has problems to explain the formation of monopolies. Even, as Friedman puts it, governments must delineate the legal framework for the gamers can compete, but avoiding any direct intervention to change the game's rules. So, how monopolies are formed during the evolution of free market? Liberalism contends that monopolies are shaped by state in many cases. However, sometimes, the natural conditions of competence may create some inevitable private monopolies. This is the lesser evil in Friedman's doctrine.

For liberals, those nations which fail in reaching mature economies are often characterized by "extractive institutions" based on the exploitation of "the Other." As the previous argument given, development is given by the type of society and the quality of its institutions. It is a truism that the "extractive institution" signals to great concentrations of power in a small minority, which exploits the resources of society in its favor. These political institutions are based on nondemocratic governments and the lack of private property. On contrary, inclusive institutions avoid to instill monopolies vesting the power in a broader way, renewing administrations according to popular voting. Unable to extract the resources of others, this model encourages the competence to strengthen the market. As a result of this, wealth and prosperity must be inevitably reached by the citizenships. Democracy as a platform where agents can negotiate with others in an atmosphere of liberty would ensure a faster and fairer redistribution of surplus (Acemoglu & Robinson, 2012).

As earlier noted, progress or failure of a nation is determined on two relevant aspects; democracy opens the doorstep toward competition, or creative destruction, which is vital for destroying any type of monopoly (private or public). All agents would compete in egalitarian conditions in favor of consumers. Competition among social institutions and bank system cemented the possibility to foster stronger networks that accelerated the growth in the democratic societies. Without "creative destruction," our economists preclude, social institutions cannot be recycled to obtain the levels of efficiency in favor of consumers. Those countries where democracy is an important cultural value are prone to the development of vigorous economies. Ethnic cleansing, civil wars, and corruption are cultural pathologies which not only balk development but a better distribution of wealth in the society.

It is safe to see, as post-Marxist scholars did, that liberalism is based on a great quandary which is posed by capitalism. Why do we over-esteem income over other cultural values?, is happiness associated to profits? Following these above questions, aboriginal tribes are pressed to accept certain cultural values that are fabricated by West, such as income, tourism, leisure and heritage, but in doing so, their living conditions are not enhanced. This means that cultural tourism as a practice should be reconsidered respecting the viewpoint of aborigines, and Western beliefs placed under the lens of scrutiny. At the time they, natives, adopt the axioms of development as a sacred truth they inevitably are in a trap (Korstanje, 2012). This is exactly one of the points discussed by post-Marxism.

## The Voice of Post-Marxism

In sharp contrast to liberals, Marxists denounce that poverty is not a problem of economy to solve with a planning calendar, but an irreversible sign of *the great theft* obscured by an ideologised capitalism. Marx acknowledged that modern economy expanded by the force of commodity exchange. Each product is fixed of a rate which exceeds the wage of workforce. This surplus is known as *"surplus value theory."* At the time, economy growths, this does not entail further profits for workers, but for capital-owners. Ideology not only obscures the real tactics of exploitation but also gives to persons a conceptual framework to redirect their loyalties toward capital-owners (Marx, 1967; 1973). Though he never supported "communism" nor any type of political praxis, his legacy still remains as the epicenter of numerous critique studies against capitalism. Paradoxically, at the time, communist countries developed their impossibility to mature in a long-term nation-building post-Marxism mushroomed over the last years. The success of capitalism was proportionally equated to its injustice for working classes. The capitalist ethos has changed the mind of citizens, who passed being part of the production machinery. As commodities, workers are exploited to congeal the mass consumption encouraged by capitalism. The big brother is an example how people enter in competetion, as commodities, to be selected and bought by others. Participants in this reality show know that only one will win, and the rest will die. *Big Brother*, for Bauman, emulates the life in capitalist societies which enhance the style of life of a small minority by producing pauperization for the whole. The modern state set the pace to the advent of liberal market to monopolize the sense of security for people. This does not mean that states are unable to keep the security, but also the market is re-channelling the consumption by the imposition of fear. If human disasters such as Katrina show the pervasive nature of capitalism which abandoned thousands of poor citizens to death, no less truth is that the "show of disaster" unbinds of responsibilities for the event. The sense of catastrophe, like death, serves to cover the inhuman nature of capitalism (Bauman, 2007; 2008).

This society only has an answer to crisis, when its economic system is at risk. Since the real reason for disaster are ignored by the allegory of death, which persisted in the media and famous TV series where technicians and forensic experts look to solve the crime, the disaster comes sooner or later (Bauman, 2011a). Most certainly, the original position of Marxism against capital paves involuntarily the pathways for its hegemony over others forms of production. This will be discussed in the next section.

## An Alternative Option, from Production to Consumption

In his seminal book *The Age of Extremes*, Hobsbawm reminds how important was the great slump for recycling and consolidating capitalism as a cultural and mega-project worldwide. The fears of new fascisms, which in the past were a product of the Great Depression in the 1930s, as well as the need to freeze communism were two of the key factors that posed excessive trust in progress and capitalist production. The "golden age" of capitalism was based on a liberal climate that supported the supremacy of technology over workforce. Reducing costs in order for gaining further profits not only became in one of the priorities of capitalist-owners, but also the main problem to face in next decades, above all after 1972. The concept of full-employment which was associated to production sets the pace to a new concept with lesser jobs but more products to consume. Invariably this led to a process of labor precaritization the vulnerated the rights of workers (Hobsbawm, 1994). The liberalization of capital, conjoined to globalization, expanded the opportunities for some countries while subsumed others in poverty and exclusion. In the passage from a society of producers to consumers, left-wind intellectuals and Marxists played a crucial role. Since particularly they were strongly concerned by the rise of poverty, which they thought was a result of certain imbalances created by producers, the right of consuming was posed as a valid solution to reduce poverty in underdeveloped and developed worlds (Donohue, 2003). In recent years, the impossibilities to struggle against poverty paved the ways to produce a new spectacle around slums and ghettos that far from solving the problem, aggravates it. To put this in bluntly, capitalism expansion is in direct proportion to the asymmetries it produces.

Returning to Hobsbawm, it is a truism that capital-owners kept the peace under the divide and rule logic. The segmentation of classes according to what they may consumer was doubtless one of the most success ideological tactics served to balk cooperation among workers. Each class not only devoted its efforts to protect their own interests, but also within working class, different consuming trends, clothes, tastes and status prevented the formation of a unified and shared conscience. The metaphor of life embodied in a youth hero who found his death at thirty years of age started a cultural revolution to enhance consumption. Since the start of the culture of revolution come from the 1960s, it forged a cult to individualism that ideologically legitimized all doctrines of consumption theory (Hobsbawm, 1994). In some respect, the links were weakened at the same time labor was considered in shortage. Hobsbawm writes, "the cultural revolution of the later twentieth century can thus best be understood as a triumph of individual over society, or rather, the breaking of the threads which in the past has woven humans being into social textures. For such textures had consisted not only of the actual relations between human beings and their forms of organization but also of the general models of such relations and the expected patterns of peoples' behaviour." (Hobsbawm, 1994: 334)

In fact, the atomization of workers not only was functional to capital owners, but allowed a climate of eternal struggle among classes to defeat the Other.

If during centuries, humankind lived from peasantry and agriculture, industrialism first and globalization later produced an expansion in profits and productions but reducing the costs at their discretion. The introduction of technology not only pressed thousands who lived from land to cities, but also pitted the worker against the worker for a simple job. However, things come worse to worsts. If the problem of poverty widely denounced by Leftist and Marxist intellectuals was a great problem for the harmonization of society, the adoption of a consumerist model will engender unexpected negative effects on modern economy. Unlike our grand-parents who lived in a productive society, we live in moment where consumption was the epicenter or main value of economic theory. Kathleen Donohue (2003) explains one of the factors that facilitated the expansion of capitalism was the passing from a productive to consuming society. Originally, the first liberal economists envisaged consumption and consumers from a pejorative perspective. Not only by the chaos and social disorganization that uncontrolled consuming generates, but also because it represents a way of destroying wealth. As Donohue acknowledges in her fascinating book *Freedom from Want*, this was until Franklin D. Roosevelt declared his four freedoms (fear, speech, religion and want). The former one, freedom from want, was not early addressed by Puritanism and Calvinism or by classical liberalism. The era of consumers and liberal consumerism was introduced by the belief the demand was more important than offer. If the economy postulated the importance of a human division of labor and production as the epicenter for the linear progress of welfare and of nations, modern consumerism upends the message. The attention is focused on poverty and its effects on social scaffolding. As Donohue writes,

"Even the classical liberals turned their attention to eradication of poverty; they continued to emphasize production rather than consumption. If one was entitled to consume only what one had produced, then, classical liberal reasoned, the only way that government could eliminate poverty was by increasing productivity." (p. 4)

Paradoxically, this paves the ways for passing from industrialism to consumerism. Not surprisingly, this paradox has questions respecting to those who would benefit from a productivity enhancement, they would be the capital-owners, who seek their multiplication of profits? or work-force more interested in protecting their wages?

This point divided the voices into two main contrasting tendencies: liberal capitalism, which was a wave interested in protecting the interest of owners; and socialism, more prone to coordinating unionization and worker claims. Elegantly, Donohue said that it was unfortunate to see how both have failed to solve this paradox.

The frenetic quest for profits led societies to adopt consumer-oriented system of productions which produced what consumers needed. This qualitative view was of paramount importance to understand the radical change America was internally facing. In doing so, the Keynesian policies fit like a glove. Strong regulatory measures as well as welfare programs disciplined the citizenship to understand the new dilemma of modern economy; consumerism is the only valid way in order for poverty to be eradicated. The classic mercantilist view of economy that characterized the "producerist" society from 1870 to 1900, established that consumption undermined the wealth of nations, but in what forms?

Starting from the premise that the wealth of nations was a question of equilibrium, economists thought that the only manner to boost the economy of a country was at the cost of another country. In this viewpoint, a strong commercial relationship among nations should be organized in view of trade. Whenever, exports supersede imports, the economy rises. Nevertheless, consumption was one of the main threats of well-being simply because it reduces the goods available for export. Here is one of the ideological pillars of modern capitalism. In the outset of twentieth century, economists formulated a curious quandary to overcome the obstacle of poverty. Even if mercantilists conceived a "regulated consumption," they neglected the thesis that consumption drives the tenets of economy. However, a new liberal trend instilled the belief that consumption drives economy, in what resulted that the only pathways for expanding prosperity was enhancing production. To accomplish this task, societies should import and develop strong capital investment accompanied by modern technological machines. Subordinated to this logic, economy compelled to the formation of extractive institutions that protected the profits of elite, while the workforce was pressed to compete for ever-decreasing, low-skilled positions. The first Marxists thought that the market gave interesting new opportunities for capital investment (by stimulating mass consumption), but reduced the genuine growth of society.

After 1940, the freedom from want was related to one of human basic needs and expanded to the world as an unquestionable principle. This was undoubtedly possible because intellectuals have discussed in earlier centuries the importance of consumption as an efficient instrument to reduce pauperism. The financial crisis in the 1930s paves the pathways for nations to embrace this paradigm without resistance. Liberals formulated "the new deal of liberalism" to transform American society, even mingling the discourse of consumption with democracy. As Donohue puts it,

"This new liberal system was not without its detractors. Critics became increasingly concerned that freedom from want was being equated with a right of plenty. And they worried that material plenty was being treated as a precondition of democracy." (p. 277)

Ideologically, Americans have felt "superior" to other nations because they are enthralled as the main democratic and prosperous society; although more egalitarian at the surface, American citizens are subject to more work and consumption but less leisure. It is important not to lose the sight that in a pro consumer society, workers are bombarded with emulation and advertising creating the needs to buy. This not only jeopardized their real liberty to choose, but also seriously affects democracy. Detractors of capitalism, left-wing scholars among them, who pushed their focus on the arbitrariness of producers, were involuntarily responsible or conducive to the formation of a global society of consumers. Those denunciations on an economy that protect the interests of producers as well as the need to adopt consumption to break the material asymmetries among classes were two guiding concepts to embrace a globalized version of capitalism, prone to mass consumption. Donohue reminds not only the myopia of Marxism to interpret capitalist evolution, but also how its criticism offered new channels for a much deeper globalized economy, or at least, the passing from a society of producers to consumers.

## The Concept of Identity

Marxists and post-Marxists claim a paradox which lies in the fact that "community" became in a buzzword precisely in an age where social ties were in decline. Citizens of the First World appeal to "identity" as something which can be changed according to their desires; not only this, but also, as Hobsbawm wrote,

> "what ethnic identity politics had in common with fin-de-siecle ethnic nation-
> alism was the insistence that one's group identity consisted in some existen-
> tial, supposedly primordial, unchangeable and therefore permanent personal
> characteristic shared with other members of the group, and with no one else.
> Exclusiveness was all the more essential to it, since the actual differences
> which marked human communities off from each other were attenuated."
> (Hobsbawm, 1994, pp. 428–429)

In the same context, Jean and John Comaroff call the attention to the problem of ethnicity in modern world, not as a precondition toward egalitarian treatment but to conflict and commoditization. The process of globalization accelerated the commoditization of culture. Since the inception of anthropology as a discipline interested in the Other, until now there has not been an epoch too prone to abo-riginality but paradoxically too distant to accept "the Other," who is mobile and in in quest of hospitality. These days, aboriginals appeal to reinforce their own differences to be sold to the international segment of travellers and tourists. In perspective, cultural tourism is one of the fastest-growing industries in the world. Ethnicity, in this vein, sets the pace to a new type of cultural consumption fab-ricated from outside to regulate emotions. The term "empowerment" as it has been formulated by the specialized literature is defined as strategy followed by local actors to improve economic and social conditions by means of their pro-active participation and commitment. Local natives adopted empowerment as a platform of escape from the oppressive condition of exploitation to which they were historically subject. Identity as a social construct plays a crucial role in the emancipation of groups which were previously relegated to peripheral positions in the economies. Basically, cultural tourism not only evokes a vibrant past which does not exist, but also confers to local communities the legal mechanism for launching to self-representation. The value of aboriginal culture is conditioned by those features that legitimate the West's supremacy. What Aboriginals like to say may be significant or not, depending on the possibilities their discourse may be commercialized to international segments. This represents a much deeper process of alienation, where cultures are disclosed from their original roots. In doing so, the culture is sold, attending only to the interests of consumers. The enthusiasm and leading role of Aboriginals as cultural managers not only blur the conflictive relations of the fourth world and states but also creates new ones. In this discussion, two significant ideas arise. On one hand, tourism disposes from cultural protection to redraw the geography of the world. On another, natives construct their sentiment of belonging in view of what tourists want to hear and see. The merit of this work consists in reminding us that this trend not only blurs the boundaries between past and present but also imposes new economies based on ethno-merchandise, where the production never ends. The classic rules of economy teach us that the rise of demand entails a decline in production. Needless to say, this does not happen with ethno-merchandise. The greater the demand for cultural consumption, the better for production; that way, the destination never declines in extractives. Those nation-states which systematically oppressed the rights of aborigines now do the same by applying exorbitant taxes to a more autonomous community which rejects being part of a shared nationhood. This engenders not only serious conflicts between local communities and states, but also paves the way for the acceleration of genocides and ethnic cleansings (Comaroff & Comaroff, 2009). This suggests the problem of heritage opens the doors for a pungent point that poses nation-states as having primary responsibility that some groups are exterminated or placed under extreme living conditions. Additionally, the sense of community was emptied to be recycled for international commercial forces that draw any intangible good such as history, culture or ethnicity into exchangeable and alienable possessions. It was in consonant with what reviews Bauman in his recent book *The Society under Siege*. Nation-states have been recycled as commodities for mega events such as football's World Cup or any other festival. The society lies on the siege of a bio politic form of control that encourages the mobilities of ones and the immobility of the rest. Since globalization blurred the boundaries between in and out, travellers have no other direction to make their journeys unless by the pseudo-reality (Bauman, 2011b).

## Reviewing Slum Tourism

The problem of poverty, undoubtedly, is a moral disaster, which not only takes a chronic nature but also it is very hard to grasp. Returning to Bauman, one must think that capitalism seems to be an asymmetrical model where almost 90%

of produced wealth is kept in the hands of a selective elite of 2% of the total population. In what is a paradoxical situation, globalization opened the doorstep for mobilities, but not for all. While only the elite is financially invested to me mobile, which means visiting any geographical points in quest of cultural exoticism or multicultural encounters, migrants are subject to extreme conditions of exploitation and pauperism. They are surveilled in order not to move from ghettos where they dwell (Bauman, 1998). Neither culture nor the ideology of mobilities does suffice to explain the uneven asymmetries between have and have-nots. Over recent years, some experts in tourism installed the discussion of poverty as a main obstacle to overcome. It was unfortunate that ghettos and slums not only are being triplicated worldwide, but also poses serious risks for the smooth operation of industry.

Like many other segments such as dark tourism, doom tourism or even disaster tourism, touring on slums offered a great opportunity in order for state to take intervention of zones otherwise remained out of control. Likewise, some scholars started to see "slum tourism" as a fertile ground to expand not only political stability but the presence of states to peripheral neighbors which lacked of the necessary infrastructure to survive (Holst, 2014). Poverty was the key factors to generate attractiveness in first-world tourists who were interested or looked for more authentic connections than classical tourism (Dürr & Jaffe 2012; Dyson, 2012; Frenzel & Koens, 2012; Mekawy, 2014; Meschkank, 2011). Self-managed by natives, slum tourism becomes in a good opportunity to poverty relief and economic revitalization. Though from diverse perspectives, specialized literature emphasizes that slum tourism helps native in the following points:

a)  Enhancing attractiveness to have further investments, which can be re-channeled toward infrastructure
b)  Giving tourists a chance to understand or critically reconsider their own lives beyond the materiality of capitalism
c)  Allowing more authentic inter-cultural encounters between hosts and guests
d)  Alleviating poverty or offering economic profits for local stakeholders
e)  Furthering tolerance of ethnic differences

Nonetheless, no less true is that he geographies of slums denote an extreme marginalization, racism and ghettoization respecting to the privileged urban landscape. In this vein, Emily LeBaron (2014) understands that although slum tourism helps residents to better their economies, social exclusion is not reverted. In Brazil, *Favelados* (dwellers of Favelas) face certain financial independence respecting to central administrations, but they do not trust tourism would be a valid option to improve their living conditions. The marketing of Favelas that encourages slum-tourism pacifies an ever-conflictive zone, where drug-dealers and crime prevail as violent practices. However, this pacification does not escape to police's corruption. Often, natives are pressed to pay for bribes and money in order for their businesses to prosper. Those who reject to collaborate with Police are hosted and jailed. Interviewees in this fieldwork evinces, LeBaron adds, though tourism serves as a fertile ground to make from Favelas a more peaceful places, in practice this never happens. Not only do *Favelados* lack original capital to conduct a tourist project, but also external groups take direct control of the necessary resources to exploit the Favelas image.

In accordance to this, Frenzel et al. (2014) explain that slum tourism as a touring practice is divided into two main destinations in the global south, Brazil and South Africa. Though its origin is not new—rather, it comes from the middle of the nineteenth century—no less true is that poverty was commoditized in order for locals to experience a process of disempowerment respecting tour operators. Neither the necessary conditions for tourist-care, nor the infrastructure given for visitors to avoid the risky reaction of other slum-dwellers, make from this segment an option that cannot be commercialized by local operators. This appears to be one of the reasons why slum tourism still is being discussed within academic circles as a paradoxical solution to poverty. As Tore Holst (2014) puts it, launching from our safer home to tour "unknown others" represents serious challenges that tourists cannot refuse. Gazing upon a dangerous "Other," slum tourism works in two directions, helping but surveilling poor natives.

In this respect, Freire-Medeiros (2014) explores the conceptual dichotomies of slum-tourism by means of her empirical fieldwork in Rocinha (Brazil). Far from being a solution to alleviate poverty, tourists replicate the conditions of exploitation local suffers in their daily life. In Favelas the nets of interactions lead to reify tourism as a mechanism to improve residents' lives, but in doing so, it produces poverty. To understand this better let us explain that in classical economy commodities are the vital part of merchandise production. In slum-tourism, the infrastructure, transport, restaurants, tour operators, tour-guides, and every service are certainly based on the pauperization. Poverty plays a crucial role as a main attraction of these types of sites. As a field-worker, she produces not only her own theory respecting to slum tourism, but also poses the polemic question whether tourism may sanitize the violence of Favelas by the imposition of market, which paradoxically reproduces poverty to attract others. Is slum tourism a result of late capitalism?

## Ecology of Disasters

George Mead, one of the fathers of symbolic interactionism, questioned why, paradoxically, many people are prone to read or listen to bad news presented by journalism, and at the time they show preference for these types of news. What is our fascination for others' suffering? He assertively concludes that the self is configured by its interactions with others. This social dialectic alludes to anticipation and interpretation as two pillars of a communication process. The self feels happiness by others' suffering, because it represents a rite necessary to avoid or think in own pain. Starting from the premise that the self is morally obliged to assist the other to reinforce its sentiment of superiority, Mead adds, this is the ethical nature of social relationship (Mead, 2009). From our viewpoint, in the neoliberal discourse life is portrayed as a race. Few will be saved while the rest are ruined. Ideologically this is not only the success of late capitalism to make people to compete with others in the market, but also this is the message of reality shows such as Big Brother, where only one can reach the glory. This cruel competition is feasible because competitors keep the faith in their own skills. Whenever one fellow falls, we feel a strange sentiment of happiness. This does not mean we are sadists, but we are glad to stay in the race. Dark tourism sites, even slum tourism, remind us how the success of the few depends upon the ruin of the whole. Slum-tourism seekers are not having a new, more authentic experience; rather, they need to witness the Other's suffering to experience a sentiment of false happiness (Korstanje, 2013; 2014b), delineating the boundaries between civilized society and backwardness. Tourists are there not to learn, but to reinforce a sentiment of supremacy which is ideologically given by *the ecology of disaster*. This will be explained with accuracy in next sections.

A wide range of studies have focused on tourism as a mechanism toward pacification or the cultural revitalization of natives and their communities (Bregha, 1989; Jafari, 1989; Litvin, 1998; Pizam, 1996). In order for the industry of tourism to grow, political stability should be ensured. Without some exceptions, tourists are natural risk-avoiders (Fuchs & Reichel, 2004; Korstanje, 2009). As Tarlow (2014) has pointed out, the tourist trip alternates two contrasting tendencies: the curiosity to experience new sensations and the sense of ontological safety. The Bible and other mythological sources reveal that the sacred space of leisure is constructed in basis of a positive precept that mandates that man relax, but at the same time, his vulnerability increases. Ancient poets and philosophers emphasized the fact that anything can happen at any time at a banquet or public game. The rise of the new modern risk and challenges for the tourism industry is what Tarlow prioritizes as the most significant aspect to debate with policy-makers. Now we are subject to a set of globalized apocalyptic risks which range from natural disasters to terrorist attacks. The attacks on the World Trade Center in 2001 represented a turning point in the security fields of the United States and the world (Tarlow, 2014). However, this begs a more than interesting question: Is risk perception a commodity used to generate attractiveness?

Legally speaking, "risk" should be defined as a process of maturation "from general to particular," which means not only that any risk refers to the risk *to* something, but also that the supposed danger is embedded in an imaginary figuration. The evaluation of risks subscribes to the doctrine of reasonable care, where the individual act is considered wrong. However, since daily social interactions triggers many risks for which the agent is not liable, it is not feasible to impugn a person for potential actions which were not committed in the present (Weinrib, 1995). Starting from the idea that risks are rooted in the future, those agents who speak on behalf of risks speak on behalf of their own interests. Most likely, this is one of the main factors that captivates analysts to describe risks.

Canadian journalist Naomi Klein (2007) alludes to the term "disaster capitalism" to observe an uncanny trend. Media and policy makers, over the last decades, have implemented programs of recovery in post disasters contexts which not only recycled the resources of economy, but engendered circles of exclusions of victims who were resituated in peripheral neighborhoods. Far from coordinating efforts to solve those glitches that lead to a state of disaster, capitalism takes the opportunity that disasters leave to conduct an economy of destructive creation (following Schumpeter's axiom). This new type of capitalism is not based on the old welfare state; it promotes disasters not only so the elite gains further legitimacy, but also so citizens accept these liberal economic policies that otherwise would be rejected. In a world where economies are globalized, Klein adds, not surprisingly, that disasters offer better opportunities for businesses and profits.

In perspective, Rodanthi Tzanelli argues convincingly that globalization plays a pervasive role by subordinating peripheral economies not only to the interests of the status quo, but to a tourist imaginary produced externally to involving natives. The spectacle not only triggers emotional reactions, but also confers an ideological message. See, for example, the case of the FIFA World Cup 2014 hosted in Brazil. Tzanelli adamantly argues that media events often strengthen the social ties of communities by homogenizing the meaning developed by history but in a context of a traumatic past, such as slavery and oppression in Brazil. Two versions of the same fabricated mythology take place in the same structure (Tzanelli, 2015a,b). Following Reijinders (2009), Tzanelli clarifies that this corresponds with the logic of "guilty landscapes" that characterizes consumption in Brazilian cities and their encounter with modernity:

> "I argue that within the same spatio-temporal frame Brazilian socio-culture becomes a flexible interpreter of its own condition and global standing. The book's two World Cup avengement teaches us that when a post-colonial culture finds itself in the late capitalism domains, it can produce different versions of the same social event in, by and for other groups." (Tzanelli, 2015b. p. 11)

This codependency between the center and its periphery can be perpetuated by an alternation of what Tzanelli dubbed as "cosmographies of riches and cosmologies of desire." The premise is that centrality can be formed by a hierarchical system of symbols, thoughts and beliefs consolidated by social networks. This remains even after post-colonial independence evoked not only by the needs of peripheral zones to be part of a sacred center, but also by a profound desire to get the foreign cosmographies of riches. Not surprisingly, this explains the periphery's fascination for tourists coming from developed nations. The original Maussian gift is exchanged between civilized and uncivilized worlds (Tzanelli, 2015a). To what extent can we be certain that this gift-exchange is not producing violence?

In earlier approaches, such as *Cosmopolitan Memory in Europe's Backwaters*, Tzanelli acknowledges that globalization and local resentment are inextricably intertwined. Based on the study case of Greece and *Mama Mia*'s destinations, she exerts a radical criticism pn "crypto-colonialism," which means the cultural encounter of first-world civilized tourists with a great variety of ethnical disputes unchecked by the former overseas periphery which was promoted by colonial legacy. Decades of exploitation of the third world prompted "an economy of victimization" which paves the ways for the advent of romantic nationalisms.

The political oppression conducted by Europe in the nineteenth and twentieth centuries created radical politics based on resentment and a suicidal redemption (as the case of terrorism evinced). These nationalisms connoted the sense of a "national pride" that produced a dichotomy between them (the enemies of the nation) and us, the good peoples. The imposition of Western archetypes by means of tourism, media and other visual allegories gives as a result a racialized habitus where the "Other" turns into a commodity (Tzanelli, 2011). She will overtly admit,

> "Neoliberalism's entropic nature appears to induce a resentment that encourages venturing out individually and destroying neighborhood reciprocities, especially where neighborly relations have always precarious. The story of adversity which affirmed my hosts self-fashioned dual habitus as Orientalized sufferers and Western civil creators, was adopted by other local enterprises that maintain or are in the process of setting up individual web pages." (Tzanelli, 2011, p. 68)

Though compellingly explained, Tzanelli's argument leaves behind the role played by disaster not only in the process of victimization, but also in the creation of national-being. Of course, as she noted, the dichotomy between them (bad) and us (good) introduces a discourse where the Other is demonized. In this vein, ethnocentrism does not precede the ethnic violence, but it is determined by a previous trauma. In other terms, moral or real disasters cause a sentiment of loss in victims who have not chosen what they face. By an arbitrary destiny, they were placed in a sad situation without their consent. The fate, god or universal forces aligned to cause serious damage to the subject. So the immediate question is "Why me, Lord?" This question has no answer. Following a natural mechanism of resilience, the community realizes after all the destruction elsewhere, there is another opportunity. Gods, despite the disasters, have protected us, or we have survived because we are stronger, smarter, superior or faster than the Other who perished. At a first stage this is natural, but if unchecked or regulated, it can wake up pathological chauvinist sentiments that lead communities or peoples to xenophobia and ethnocentrism. This is a type of psychological narcissism produced by the disaster. If this pathological behavior is not corrected, victims over-valorize not only their imaginary skills and potentialities, but also feel that happiness can be reached only through pain (producing the epicenter of the ascetic personality). This was evinced by my last fieldwork conducted in a disaster-spot in Chile as well as by some interviews over "*descendientes de desaparecidos*," relatives of "disappeared peoples," during the last bloody dictatorship from 1976 to 1982. Symbolically invested by a divine touch, survivors feel they are part of something important, and this is the reason why romanticism or nationalisms resulted from deep stages of crisis or disasters. We agree that globalization or capitalism enlarges some already-existent cleavages of peripheral nations exploited by the colonial legacy. To my knowledge the point of discussion lies in how late-capitalism instills this narcissism to weaken the social ties of community, recycling their forms of traditions and interactions into commodities. Once done, as Tzanelli observed, natives are offered to international tourism demands as products. The concept of supremacy of one ethnicity over others is determined *by the ecology of disaster*.

In what way might disasters be conducive to the exploitation of cultural tourism? In this respect, Comaroff and Comaroff have denounced that cultural tourism is paving the way for ethnic cleansing and genocides. Though they do not specify why, consider a pristine aboriginal community which was subject to an unspeakable cruelty by colonial powers. Now, this community may gain financial independence for their current nation-state if tourism is accepted as a primary means of poverty relief. Secondly, the West will develop a romantized imaginary of these exploited aborigines. They will develop this above-described sentiment of ethnocentrism, which will result in a direct struggle with the nation-state for the monopolization of resources (Comaroff & Comarroff, 2009).

However, as a project capitalism does not prosper when social ties are undermined. Bauman was correct in alerting us to the fact that that today, consumers have irreversibly turned into consumed objects, commodities to be sold to those who can pay (Bauman, 2007). Let's explain this with clarity in the conclusion.

## Conclusion

Capitalism should be understood as a cultural project, besides an economic system, which is based on two preliminary aspects: social Darwinism and the doctrine of predestination enrooted in the Protestant spirit. Two scholars have explored with brilliant mastery on both, Max Weber (2012) and Richard Hofstadter (1963). While the former signaled to capitalism as a consequence of Protestant Reform that divorced from the Catholic Church, the latter envisaged that social Darwinism was the key factor to grant the competence necessary for market expansion. Social Darwinism was a theory coined by Sir. Francis Galton, whose interests were oriented to adapt the concept of the "evolution of species," as it has been delineated by Charles Darwin, to the social world. However, Galton not only misjudged Darwin's advances in the fields of biology but also confused "the survival of the fittest," with "the survival of strongest." In contrast to Darwin, social Darwinism observed that natural selection can be applied to social scaffolding: some species struggle with the environment to survive; humans struggle with others to reach success. In this respect, the Anglo race was placed on the top of the social pyramid as the most evolutionary ethnicity with respect to other minorities. At the same time, this doctrine paved the way not only for racist ideas in America that shaped capitalism, but also for Nazism in Europe. In parallel, as Hofstadter puts it, the idea of a privileged race, or dreams of an uphill city, contributed to a discourse of superiority of Anglo-Saxons over other cultures, which sooner or later encouraged "the war of all against all"; social Darwinism works because rank-and-file workers struggle with other workers for a job or better opportunities. While capital-owners monopolize their power into few hands, the workforce is divided to avoid unionization. Those who have not developed adaptive skills to survive are considered "the weak." After all, capitalism always grants the survival of the strongest, the best agent. In the field of religion, Weber anticipated a similar landscape.

Capitalism was the result of the Protestant logic of "predestination," which means that the soul's salvation was predetermined by God in the Book of Life. Only a few will be gathered by the Lord in the final days. For wayward Protestants, the world not only is a dangerous place, but also the platform to show one deserves salvation. The force of labor seems to be the sign marking the boundaries between doomed and saved souls. This is the main cultural difference between Catholics and Protestants.

In a recent book entitled *A Difficult World: Examining the Roots of Capitalism*, I have continued the discussion by adding a new element, the ecology of disaster. Starting with the premise that the times of Hofstadter and Weber have gone forever, I argue that capitalism has been enlarged to the contours of this world. Though social Darwinism remains in the core of markets, no less true is that disasters are conducive to the ultimate logic of capital. Tzanelli did the correct thing in confirming that resentment was the symbolic core of national-being, but he left out the role of risk-perception in the process. Disasters produce a lot of victims, who are involuntarily in a situation they would never choose. In order to overcome the trauma by starting with the process of resiliency, survivors believe they have been protected by gods, or have survived by their natural skills. Despite the extreme loss, they feel not everything is lost. And of course, they have survived because of their strengths. Although this sentiment is natural during a temporal time-frame, whenever there is not direct intervention of therapists, chauvinists or xenophobic acts may surface. This is the reason not only why media are strongly interested in covering news of disasters, but also why ethnic conflicts have increased. Capitalism disorganizes the social trust among citizens by the installation of the allegory of superman, a special personage whose powers make him outstanding with respect to humans. Of course, poverty, in other words, is a chronic disaster which affects thousands of peoples who are daily relegated from this paradise created by Anglo-Protestant ethos where only few selected peoples can dwell. This way of thinking, however, creates serious asymmetries precisely in the contours. The hermeneutic circle between exploited and exploiters has been fulfilled by new trends of tourism, which stimulate the consumption of authentic cultures (Korstanje, 2015). Slum tourism, far from giving a solution for the problem, replicates those conditions of exploitation that aggravate poverty. In the same way, we have already observed that just as journalism captivates the attention of its audience in order to strengthen their self-esteem (or sentiment of supremacy), slum-tourists reinforce their own sentiments of civility over the Barbarian World. As earlier discussed, life is seen as a great race where only one can be the winner. From *Big Brother* to *The Hunger Games*, this is the ideological rule that characterizes the postmodern world. Those stragglers who lag behind as slum-dwellers are considered weak or unworthy of salvation; in the same way, to convert workers into commodities, capitalism needs to disorganize social trust. In so doing, the sense of uniqueness plays a vital role in leading toward narcissism. Contextually, slum tourism revitalizes the need to on gaze Other's suffering to feel one might be special. As earlier discussed, to what extent tourism or slum tourism are valid options to pacify conflictive hot-spots is a point which merits much deeper research by the academy.

# 3 Consuming Disasters

## Introduction

At 2:46 p.m. on March 11, 2011, Japan suffered one of its most intense and devastating earthquakes. The earthquake measured 7.9 on the Richter scale. It was so intense that the world's media provided almost nonstop 24-hour news coverage. The reports spoke about the number of victims, and behind the reports the ghost of a Chernobyl-like nuclear disaster was ever present. The earthquake followed by a tsunami not only devastated the Japanese coast but also posed serious risks should the Fukushima nuclear reactor have suffered a meltdown. Such a meltdown was a more serious threat to life, considering the following relevant aspects.

- The potential for a nuclear accident or worse now became a real possibility, such as a repetition of what occurred in Chernobyl. This potential nuclear threat dominated the public's anguish.
- No one was sure what would be the negative results on the locale's children.

- Humanity once again had to note that in the face of the earthquake and tsunami it was powerless.

- Television viewers saw the harm that nature had done both on the land and in the sea.
- Television viewers in other countries realized that no one was immune from the uncontrollable effects of a natural disaster, thus viewers once again noted their impotence in the face of natural disasters. For example, the mass media showed pictures of water invading Japanese cities and destroying all that lay in its path.
- The media's emphasis on personal "miracles" not only reinforced the notion of impotence in the face of natural disasters but also introduced an element of the mystical into the tragedy. Media reports of people who saved their lives against all odds served not only as examples of the exception to the rule, but also introduced an element of humility into the arrogance of modernity. Science simply could not solve everything, and once again we noted the concept of deus ex machina.
- The story was brought home by eyewitness accounts of visitors to Japan.

Quarantelli (2006), a senior sociologist who devoted his life to themes of disasters, revealed that the way people perceive the world has changed. In place of classical disasters, as narrated by cinema, another type of new, virtualized disaster has emerged. This new type of disaster indexes events which never happened in reality. Based on suppositions, speculations and hypotheses, these new types of "mediated" disasters have become cultural entertainment. Quarantelli's assertion led me (Korstanje 2011a,b) to argue that we are living at the end of resiliency, because our ability to learn from events is being undermined. Any virtual disaster not only sets the pace for others, but the boundaries between reason and cause become blurred. The more apocalyptic, more intriguing and more striking the virtualized disasters, the more they pose a challenge to science. A careful review of the media accounting of natural and man-made disasters demonstrates that the media often have their own agenda. For example, although officially denied, a careful observer will note that the media's experts often seem to have predetermined roles. Their scripts demonstrate that the media hosts not only guide the expert's message, but should the expert go off script, s/he faces being cut off. Media personalities not only control the microphone but also give themselves a sense of self-importance. Thus, news often becomes a spectacle in and of itself. Television reporting often becomes a mixture of sensationalism mixed with scientific truth in which media personalities create an apocalyptic image. The report leaves the viewer with the sensation that the worst is yet to come. If we apply this principle to the case of Japan, we can note how the media spoke about the possibility of a "nuclear Armageddon." However, just as in the majority of other disaster stories, although the case of the potential "nuclear catastrophe" may have had us on the edge of our seats for a while, this threat vanished as the media turned its attention elsewhere.

Jean Baudrillard was one of the philosophers who have devoted their attention to the study of fear and media. His legacy poses the question in a serious debate considering not only how reality is built, but also how disasters are covered and interposed. Baudrillard's insight influenced my approaches (Korstanje, 2010), as I recently studied the connection between disasters and the emergence of a new resilience in cultural studies. Stimulating a fertile ground to discuss to what extent the media created a parallel reality, enrooted in the uncertainty of future, Baudrillard reminds us that in the absence of a clear diagnosis of reasons for a state of emergency, it is impossible to establish successful plans for risk mitigation. Any attempt to reduce risks in the real world will create new, unplanned risks, according to the principle of reversibility. Secondly, the attacks perpetrated against the World Trade Center (WTC) represent the success of the individual over the world of cloning. The WTC or the Twin Towers are alike, as cloned from the same model (Baudrillard, 2003). Any suicide exhibits the last individual effort at self-annihilation in the world of hyper-reality. Like buildings, news reports are copied and distributed to a broader audience, which is pressed to live in an eternal present. If causes and effects are blurred in the same setting, one disaster will set the pace for the others, undermining our capacity to learn from tragedies. Nationalism and patriotism play a pervasive role, Baudrillard admits, because they achieve the social cohesion in the context of uncertainty or emergency, and obscure enough of the disaster so as to be repeated again, and again.

In this book I present culture and travel as two important elements in trying to comprehend the relationship between disasters and consumption. By means of content analysis as a principle methodology, this study uses a letter sent by the FCAJ (Spanish acronym for "Argentine–Japanese Cultural Foundation"), with its main offices in Buenos Aires' Japanese Gardens district. In the letter the FCAJ invited its members to make a cultural journey to Japan soon after the earthquake. This essay uses this letter to explore the different narratives that comprise the cultural axis of a trip—an aspect rarely studied within the academic literature. Tourism philosophy is presented as a useful tool to figure out questions attached to the symbolic elaboration of misfortune and how tourism deals with human and natural misfortunes.

It is not uncommon that during emergencies or natural disasters a number of social psychological triggers come to the forefront and place the event in a comprehensible context. Without these social psychological triggers the public would be left in an anomic state, and social disintegration would set in. Two ways we sort out and make sense of such tragedies are through the twin social mechanisms of nationalism and consumerism. During moments when societies face existential crises, survival may depend on strengthening individuality and group identity. These two social phenomena act as antidotes to the tragedy and allow for group survival. Thus, after a tragedy such as a tsunami or earthquake, national or group pride facilitates the social healing process. It is against this backdrop that we analyze the media coverage and the reaction of the Buenos Aires Japanese community to the earthquake and tsunami that struck Japan in 2011 and the dangers that ensued from the damage to the Fukuyima reactor. Although this work is about one small community within the Japanese diaspora, its social psychological insights are not confined to this community, but should be replicable throughout the world.

The main thesis in this work is that both tourism and nationalism operate as ideological instruments so as not to fragment the nation. Beyond the trauma and suffering, the survivor develops an exaggerated self-image that leads to ethnocentrism and chauvinism. After all, survivors have passed the proof of death. Their invulnerability is often accompanied with stories linked to strength, fate, pride and courage. This sentiment, which in the short run helps people to overcome the wounds post-disaster, at a later time becomes an iron cage, because it upends the causes and consequences of the event. As a consequence, those responsible for the event elude their responsibility. As Baudrillard (2002) claimed, in a world where the events have been emptied and transformed in pseudo-events, disasters are commoditized to entertain a much broader audience.

## The Attractiveness of Mobility

Currently, travel and mobility have been transformed into two of modernity's complementary activities. Not only has travel increased, but also the speed in which we travel has increased. Connected to this increase, but not necessarily due to it, humanity's capacity to transmit information across the world has also increased (Birtchnell & Buscher, 2011; Giddens, 1991; Lash & Urry, 1998; Lew, 1987; Urry, 2007; Virilio, 1991; 2007). This increase in both the transmission of information and the increase in travel, while not irrevocable, is hard to stop. Although governments in countries such as China, Iran and Syria have worked hard to stop the flow of information, their populations have found new and innovative ways to absorb the ever-increasing flow of cross-border information.

Respecting travel mobility, often the number of trips made have to do with types of dangers associated with the place to where the trip is to be made or the type of trip. Dangers may include such things as terrorism, diseases, crime and natural disasters. Tourist trips facilitate the convergence of fear and social class distinction (Douglas 1997). There is no trip without the possibility of an accident. Despite the risks involved, people do not shy away from travel because they falsely believe that they can avoid all risks. It should be noted that the risk of accidents, and above all the inherent thrill of danger, is a determining factor in how adventurous a trip is perceived to be. This is one reason that people may travel to places that are known for being off the beaten path. For example, a volcano's eruption may constrict demand for its locale for a while, but once the danger has been removed, the destination often becomes even more popular. Tourism destinations, be they places where there have been battles or disasters, or have emerged as a product of a previous accident, often become tourism beacons. (Bianchi, 2007; Kaelber, 2007; Korstanje, 2010; Lennon and Folley, 2000; O'Rourke, 1988; Poria, 2007; C. Ryan, 2005; Seaton, 1996; 1999; 2000; Stone, 2005; 2011; Urry, 2001).

In an interesting manuscript, George, Inbakaran, and Poyyamoli (2010) emphasize that tourism is different from other kinds of travel. Travel takes us from one place to another, but tourism is circular, and the goal is to visit a place and then return; it is a trip that takes us to where we began. One tourism motivation is curiosity. The sense of danger inherent in any tourism experience leads to both adventure and excitement. Paradoxically, we search for safe places in which to stay and it is the industry's responsibility to maximize the traveler's security, permitting a sense of danger and excitement at the same time. Elías and Dunning (1992), on the other hand, note that we classify business or pleasure trips by a sense of a controlled environment that separates us from fear. A limited dose of fundamental risk provides a social distinction. One aspect of tourism is that it dislocates our sense of belonging and our identity by placing us in an anomie (Tang and Wong, 2009).

The German philosopher Wenge proposes three theories to explain the reasons we travel: (1) we seek to evade something, (2) we seek some form of status, or (3) we go on a pilgrimage. In the first case, that of evasion, Wenge suggests that we seek travel to separate ourselves from life's routine and drudgery. The traveler seeks relief from work that both alienates and oppresses. Using this perspective, we see a convergence of the aspiration for something new with the desire to get away from life's daily routines. In Wenge's second case, the thesis of conformity or status, says that we travel to fit into the norms of the dominant class from which comes the ostentatious consumption of experiences and social recognition, a kind of conspicuous consumption (Veblen, 1899). Finally, travel as pilgrimage refers to the need for movement and implies obligation and exhibition. In the modern world pilgrimages often interconnect with messages that the media send forth. Thus, what we read in a novel or see on television or in movies becomes a tourist pilgrimage, of either the secular or religious variety. For example, a visit to many of the monuments in Washington, DC, can be a secular pilgrimage. In like manner, many people wanted to visit the train station from which Harry Potter left for the mythical world of Hogwarts School of Witchcraft and Wizardry or the churches mentioned in Dan Brown's *Da Vinci Code* (Wenge, 2007). Wenge does not clarify whether his pilgrimage thesis is a matter of underlining social fault lines or an exhibitionist form of being different. On this point Korstanje and Busby (2010) have explained the origin of tourism may be from the Biblical contexts where sin implies a movement outside of the norms as a form of evasion of responsibility. The Hebrew verbal root for the verb "to sin" (*chet-tet-alef*) literally means to miss the mark or for the arrow to miss its target.

In agreement with the above authors, Larsen (2007; 2009) introduces a new category, which he calls "worry," as a form of normative reinforcement. Worry is an inference that transcends the cognitive field exclusively with the appearance of probable results, coupled with a person's or group's negative energy that created a desire for travel. Worry is related to danger. Furthermore, as worry increases, there is a decline in our willingness to assume risks. For this reason travelers have greater worries when they are at home imagining their trip in comparison to when they are on a trip (Larsen, 2007; 2009). In recent decades, professional advice has become a way for people to seek an efficient way to put threats into intellectually understandable contexts. The travel professional has been become the go-to person in order to obtain technical advice and to measure risk. Professionals are precisely those who are empowered by society (or in some places the state) to protect individual's lives to maximize earning and reduce dangers (Bledstein, 1978; Beck, 2006; Bauman, 2008).

In the case of tourism, the professional's familiarity with potential dangers sends a reassuring message to the client, giving her/him a certain sense of security that s/he can take on the trip. (Fielding et al., 2005). Moving beyond the field of travel we note that Sjoberg considers that there exists a differentiation in the way in which an expert analyzes a threat in contrast to public opinion. For example, a professional who is dedicated to a nuclear threat will view the threat through the lens of his knowledge base and in a different way from that of someone with a lesser knowledge. This type of knowledge is often called high knowledge as opposed to low knowledge. A person may have high knowledge in one area but in other areas only low knowledge. There is no consensus in the literature on this point. For example, there are studies that demonstrate that in the field of medicine both doctors and patients perceive high levels of risk in the face of high potential for illnesses. According to Thomas Kuhn (1962), experts are often committed to the paradigm of their discipline, and therefore hold on to this belief with a high level of confidence. To be an expert is to believe in one's ability to grapple with, and seek ways to treat, the problem. Politicians, on the other hand, must react to public trends and therefore tend to hold much lower confidence levels.

There are two roles that experts play in the management of risk: protector and promoter. The first type refers to the professionals who are part of the public information services with the goal of informing the public so as to avoid states of emergency. Protectors tend to be upset that the public may have scarce information about a determined risk, and these experts will put their efforts into shaping the debate regarding specific social questions—for example, doctors, first aid workers or experts in natural disasters. Their desire to shape the debate may mean that the so-called experts may become part of the problem. In much of the population there exists the perception that there is a relationship between technology and risk, a pessimistic perspective which signals that technology is responsible for the risk.

The sociologies of Beck (2006) and Giddens (1991) have examined the relationship between technology and risk. From Beck's perspective, the means of production of modern society is ever changing even when it is in the world of "as if" or "might be." Beck argues that societies feign practices and customs from previous decades, even when the market and its forms of production have changed direction. In the social world we observe a preliminary state that stands between an industrial society and a risk society. The globalization of risk assaults the individual's integrity. Beck is conscious that the process of modernity regressed soon after the Chernobyl accident in the Ukraine. Chernobyl altered radically the way in which we perceive risk and threats. These post-Chernobyl risks differ from the risks that medieval travelers faced. The medieval traveler evaluated his personal risks before setting forth on his/her adventure. Modern risks, on the other hand, are presented not on the micro scale but rather on the macro scale, such as global risks, world catastrophes and chaotic situations in which the traveler is enveloped in a sense of impotency (Beck, 2006).

According to Beck, minor threats or individual risks eventually become tolerated by society, but as these risks accumulate they become major threats. For example, the random murder of innocent civilians by terrorist groups in places such as Israel is often tolerated by the world, but when the numbers become such that Israel takes action, then the individual tragedies of rocket attacks on schoolchildren become international threats to world peace, and the United Nations becomes involved. The saying that the destruction of even one life is the destruction of an entire world has now been lost to the modern media. In this way, as opposed to the business class that maintains a strict line of separation between economic classes, modern society confronts a new configuration in its social order. This new society receives the name "risk society," whose principal characteristic lies in the risks that are equally distributed throughout the classes and social groupings (Beck, 2006). Against the logic of material appropriation of merchandise, we now are presented with the antithesis: the logic of denial. By means of selective journalism, privileged groups hide information about risks and minimize the collateral damage produced by hyper-consumption. Responsibilities and rights blur the borders between innocence and culpability. From this perspective, risk production is proportional to the distribution of wealth. Beck's main thesis is that the imposition of risks on the consumer involves the idea of a limited stimulation by the market. From this perspective, fear is the only necessity that has no end point, and there is always room for more (Beck, 2006). As production increases so do risks.

Anthony Giddens proposes to understand modernity and technology as an epistemological break that is divorced from ideals to the point of creating fragmentation and uncertainty. According to Giddens, capitalism needs a degree of risk to maintain its raison d'être. The mediation of capital fulfills a primordial role in the configuration of risk, as it absorbs the dangers derived from fear. For example, an insurance company that assumes third-party risks demands a specific amount of money as compensation. Traditional societies are nourished by trust in the past while at the same time blurring the past. In a like manner, modern technology has eroded religion, even to the point of transforming itself into its own god. Thus, we observe that experts have replaced priests in the selling of fear. In the Christian world the notion of Hell has been replaced by modernity's use of risk (Giddens, 1991; 1999a; 2000).

According to Leo Marx (1994) the conception of technology during the Enlightenment began to change radically with the arrival of modernity. The Enlightenment created a utopian ideal with respect to progress, but technology played a limited role in its relationship to this ideal. With modernity, the relationship became reversed creating a technocratic and technological truth in which technology begins to subvert the Enlightenment's ideals. Postmodernism criticizes the use given to technology by the Enlightenment. Postmodern critics argue that if these goals rest only in the technical then these goals are amoral and irrational in and of themselves. From its creation, soon after the French involvement in its Vietnam War, postmodernism has been pessimistic regarding the use and role of technology. It rejects not only the Enlightenment's ideals concerning technology, but also the narrative constructed around the notion of historical progress. Nevertheless, there is an internal contradiction in that postmodernism offers a much more technological vision than that which it aims to destroy. This contradiction holds especially true in the excessive role that the communication industry has taken in this process. In its diehard criticism of ideology and the system of ideas, postmodernism demonstrates multiple contradictions (L. Marx, 1994, p. 25).

Pippin expands this line of reasoning when he writes that if the first Marxists (including Karl Marx) considered technology as a leap backwards in the course of a society's progress, it was after the intervention of Lukacs and especially after the Frankurt School that technology began to be seen as an instrument of alienation within capitalist sociology (Pippin, 1994, p. 99). On the other hand, it was clear that technologies, such as medical technology, supported dominant groups with respect to risk. Nevertheless, it is undeniable that with the decline of technology we have seen the decline of the basis of scientific authority. Fragmentation of knowledge accompanied by an anomie of established norms resulted in an increase in each society's threshold of uncertainty. Fear is determined by the degree of narcissism developed by the self.

According to Christopher Lasch (1991), there exists an almost irreversible tendency to conceive of the external world as dangerous, catastrophic and/or chaotic. This tendency is a product of changing values and a cosmic vision that appeared for the first time in modernity. The current situation is despite the political rhetoric, that no one really seeks a solution to potentially catastrophic problems, but rather stresses individual survival. Lasch argues that in a narcissistic culture that elevates the "I" it is hard to understand the future of the "we." Modern culture shows a a lack of interest in the past and lacks a sense of tradition. In a narcissistic culture, the past represents only a trivial form of commercialization and exchange. At the same time, fear has been converted into a way for therapists to make money. Moderns have subordinated all of their inhibitions to "the company" and are incapable of satisfying their own needs. Personal self-fulfillment is presented as the maximum measure of success in a narcissistic society. There exists an entire cultural critique that holds that psychological therapy tends to indoctrinate the lower classes into upper-class goals, such as personal development and self-control. Modern society and its productive system appeal to a division of social relations and subsuming them before technical and expert dominance (Lasch, 1991).

## The Spectacle of Disasters

Scaremongering, explains Berbeglia, comes out of a double tendency to reconcile opposites. On one hand, there is fear, while on the other hand there is hope. Both stake their claim in reconstructing a new form of linkage between members of a society. The imposition of panic by means of multiple mechanisms is complemented by political messages whose ultimate ends are indoctrination and control. If on one hand scaremongering emphasizes worst-case scenarios, on the other hand it provides sufficient security to present a solution to the problem. In this way threats that promise to destroy civilization converge with possible solutions as presented by science and its community of experts. Catastrophes imply a cultural rupture, produced by human intervention in nature or by nature itself, in which humans either adapt or perish. Catastrophic events generate discussions that serve as warnings, and alternate between hope and fear. For those who follow plans, such as evacuation plans, there is hope, and for those who choose to ignore these plans or disobey them, fear is ever present. Examples of this hope/fear continuum are hurricane warnings given along the Gulf Coast. Residents are routinely told to follow evacuation orders or they risk death. The Katrina disaster that struck the city of New Orleans in 2005 versus that of Hurricane Isaac demonstrates the political symbolic construct of a disaster (Berbeglia, 2002).

Another scholar, Žižek (2011), discusses the paradox of a modernity in which certain things are permitted, but only when they link people with mobility and technology while prohibiting other things that would lead us to question the foundations of capitalism. In keeping with Žižek's argument, our world allows us to get to the moon as tourists, but it is not permitted for us to break with the ideas of the bourgeois or with a distorted idea of modern democracy. In short, experts' roles and the content that they produce only aids the market's ideological machinery. In his *Blaming the Victim*, William Ryan (1971) showed the subtle tactics used by capitalist elites to avoid facing responsibility for their decisions. Ideology serves as a system of belief that preserves the power of elites. These types of ideas are a distortion of reality, reflecting intentional purposes. Blaming the victim seems to be an ideological process that distorts the real causes of emergencies. If, for instance, and in keeping with Gandhi, poverty is a state of disaster, in American society the poor are blamed for their socioeconomic condition. The social forces that generate these unfair situations not only are not criticized but also are preserved. The difference between assistance or charity versus subordination becomes blurred if not erased in the blaming-the-victim strategies. In this respect, blaming the victim happens with exceptionalist frameworks that are applied on universal values. Whenever journalists or other analysts point out that poverty is a reason for disasters, the blaming-the-victim strategy is used to negate their analyses (W. Ryan, 1971, pp. 16–17). It is safe to affirm that social problems and disasters play a vital role in configuring the ideological discourse to blame the victims for the events.

If, as Baudrillard suggests, we are living in a time of the decline of the nation-state and of religion, its resurgence can be explained after a natural tragedy occurs. Nationalism constructs a discourse to feed its own logic in the face of adversity, chaos, anarchy and disorders. Nature is neither tamable nor always understood, and we often perceive it as hostile. Yet there are symbols that offer hope in this desolate social and political environment. Hope is often found in symbolism. For example, the figure of the rescue dog trained to save human lives transforms the harshness of nature. The Chilean or Swiss rescue dog inspires patriotism, and these nations' citizens wave their flags in unison as a sign of pride. Symbols can also be human: for example, the Israeli medical teams that came to Haiti's aid before any other nation and within some forty-eight hours had tent hospitals up and running. They created a great sense of pride in Israel. The theme there was as Europe and the American nations talked, Israel acted. Far from having disappeared, nationalism and the nation-state appear to have been transformed and are doing quite well.

Another example is that Chilean nationalism became activated in the face of the earthquake that occurred there during the end of February 2010. Words such as "courage," "uprising" and "battle" appear in the testimonies of the survivors as well as in the announcers' voices or those of the commentators who came on the air. Survivors served their society by helping to construct a national feeling to give testimony to the event. This testimony is necessary for the national dialogue that permits healing. The same phenomenon can be found both in both the Jewish world and in Germany after World War II. However, no such dialogue took place in France, and so the nation never healed. France has no equivalent to writers such as Ellie Weisel and only now, some 60 years later, is coming to terms with its political earthquake.

In post modernity, the event succumbs before the logic of the spectacle, and is transformed into a nonevent. By transforming the event into a media tale, the story comes to symbolize the lack of real events and becomes the production of nonevents. The September 11, 2001, attack against the Twin Towers inaugurated the end of history and the re-elaboration of potentiality. The media decided which events became facts and transmitted daily thousands of similar events which numb the senses and make the unique common. This same method is used by academics who produced so many ostensibly scholarly articles that they succeed in dumbing down society. Ever since SARS and until 9/11, the concept of efficiency has created a system of functional nonevents for a market that produces ever greater amounts of gradually subjective publicity (Baudrillard, 1995a; 1995b; 2001; 2002). Modern capitalist society lives under two cultural principles: the proliferation of the computer and a high degree of sexuality as expressed in the media. Threats mobilize resources with the end of legitimizing the social order. AIDS, terrorism, crack deals and electronic viruses all put into play a process whereby society examines a whole series of processes and speculations that people may have on one of these subjects.

The event creates a break between "the before and the after"; the succession of events are the result of history. Extreme phenomena acquire great virulence to the extent that they falsify human tools that are destined to the examination of the internal world and its surroundings. Baudrillard argues that humans need catastrophes so as not to be lost in emptiness or absolute nothingness. Baudrillard writes: "The total catastrophe would be that of the omnipresence of all information, of that which is totally transparent whose effects are luckily eclipsed by the computer virus. Thanks to it (the virus) we will not go on a straight line until the end of information and communication which would be death" (Baudrillard, 2000, p. 16).

The catastrophe has turned into a kind of tool with the end of avoiding the worst. In emergencies and catastrophes danger paralyzes our social lives to elude a state of disintegration. Global threats function as a virus taken from the physical body, as a fact or event X, which then moves to be virtually disseminated to other bodies from which it can infect other organisms. The mass media function is a perfect mechanism or vector to make the disaster spread. Baudrillard goes on to say that "electronic viruses are the expression of information's homicidal transparency throughout the world. AIDS is the emanation of the homicidal transparency of sexual liberation on group scales. The stock market Cracks are the expression of murderous transparency of the economy between itself, of the rapid circulation of values that are the base of both liberations from production and interchange. Once liberated, all of the processes enter into super-fusion on the scale of nuclear fusion that is its prototype" (Baudrillard, 2000, p. 42).

Given the right conditions, political manipulation proposes an objective, an evil, a problem that only it can solve or exorcize. The superiority of certain groups to define good or evil is accompanied by an ideological conversation whose maximum tool is the diffusion of fear. However, to differentiate himself from Beck, Baudrillard admits that we have weakened quite a lot in creating Satanic energy, which implies that evil has been stripped of its symbolic function. It no longer acts as a deterrent, but as a fetish blurring the limits about which we should fear. This fear does not have an objective. It is similar to an existentialist anguish. The Western world lives in a protected capsule, not unlike riding in a pressured airplane capsule, and terrorism is implicit in the effect of depressurizing. Violence practiced on the East turns against the West, which reciprocally weakens ethical and moral values.

Baudrillard calls attention to the fact that threats mobilize resources with the end of legitimizing society's order. AIDS, terrorism, financial and stock market crisis and electronic viruses put into play a process whereby society reviews a series of procedures and assumptions that touch upon a specific theme. The event creates a break between a "before" and an "after," and linking these events becomes history. Extreme phenomena acquire greater sensitive virulence to the measure that they become sophisticated human tools destined for the exploitation of the internal and surrounding world. Catastrophes become a tool with the end of avoiding something worse that might happen. The pursuit of manufactured events erases the principle of reality in the mind of the media.

Coulter (2012) says that Baudrillard proposes a new concept of reality based on Greek philosophy in the form of an allegory of the second law of thermodynamics, which prevents reversibility for certain processes. Any social structure, like empires, is subject to the possibility to collapse because of its own strength. If the linear evolution of technology implies moving forward to a next stage, reversibility evokes poetics as a form of displaced dialectics (Coulter, 2012). Of course, as post-structutalist Baudrillard knows, the virtualization of the media blurs the distinction between fiction and truth. Unlike other philosophers, he does not look to the truth of events. What today people know about history is by means of movies. This reveals certain ignorance about the past, but the history has ended. Starting from the premise, reversibility is a natural antidote against determinism. Baudrillard argues that poems come from ambiguity and uncertainty, which are rooted in the language. Like truth, language determines the boundaries of being, in which any meaning is subject to proper understanding. Alluding to the metaphor of "precogs" in *The Minority Report* (Dick, 2002 [1956]), who anticipated the crime before it was committed, Baudrillard's most intriguing point of debate is that fiction, like theory, give sense in order for us to understand the world. The construction of concepts reveals that nothing can be said about events. Therefore, visual appearances seem to replace meanings of the past. The vertigo of interpretation imposed by the media is based on an immediate future; it also destroyed the history. Coulter adds that we are not able to find the truth simply because it remains hidden from human cognition and it is accessible only by means of fiction. However, fiction cannot be empirically verified. After all, truth is only an illusory construction designed in order for human beings to reach nothing. The truth is like the fish that bites its own tail. Therefore, Baudrillard is convinced that 9/11 never existed. He is not the philosopher of nonsense, as some other scholars proposed. Baudillard's legacy consists in a sharp criticism against modernity and hyper-reality, to the extent of defying compliance with the market in science. Hyper-reality of the media has paved the way to create a show to be sold to an international audience where the reason and the effects of disasters are presented. As reality is not necessary in modern times, history has been commoditized to work together with nationalism and patriotism. Philosophers should distance themselves from the illusory nature of patriotism and tradition.

## Contributions of Jean Baudrillard to the Understanding of Reality

Baudrillard criticized the work of Susan Sontag and Noam Chomsky, arguing both were moved by certain chauvinist interests. Sontag, he said, begins with a false and mediated solidarity with humanitarian gestures in the Balkans, but these acts not only are not real, they also are counter-productive for the goals she claims to pursue. Sontag, to some extent, acts in complicity with the status quo. The splendid coverage she receives represents hypocrisy and a hidden patriotism that does not deviate from American partisanship (Baurdillard, 1985; 1986). What intellectuals do not appreciate is that terrorists do not hate the United States because it is the freest, most prosperous, wealthiest and most democratic republic of the world in which values are incidentally imposed by means of war and violence. More importantly, terrorists get their weapons, tactics, and strategies from the United States. Baudrillard explains how hate is caused by humiliation, not by exploitation. The United States and the West, especially Britain and France, colonized the Middle East mind long ago. The events of 9/11 exhibit a response to the humiliation inflicted by global powers. Neither Sontag nor Chomsky seems to realize they are using suffering to propagate American values in the world. Their inability to see the problem of democracy, or Anglo-American democracy, as well as the asymmetries given by globalization, allude to a much broader change in the means of production, as the nation-state and capitalism are inextricably intertwined.

Another interesting viewpoint comes from Paul Virilio (2010) who complemented the thoughts of Baudrillard. Is technology responsible for human disasters? Virilio says that technologies and mobilities not only have created new forms of displacements, but also have blurred the relation between time and space. As a result of this, people have full access to any geographical point of the globe in hours. The time of waiting has changed forever. Travelers now are moved by visual consumption. There is no genuine contact in visited lands. Events in the past formed history as a continuation of ordered facts, but global transportation and communication technologies make a new kind of real time in which people can no longer synchronize watches. Citizens have been transformed into consumers. History has been emptied into a fragmentation of events, dispersed globally and broadcast repeatedly. The function of the modern university is no longer the production of knowledge. Now the university is producing experts conducive to the actuarial concerns of the insurance industry and various market demands. Virilio argues that everything happens at the same time in hyper-reality, without a logical sequence. The world stage is represented outside the planet, in an exo-earth. The days of science, as an all-encompassing instrument based on rational understanding, have changed. Science has been transformed in an exo-science that promotes the simultaneous globalization of fear, whilst biology and astronomy are eclipsed by the eternal present. Virilio emphasizes the mea culpa of science for its failure to create an ethic of life. Based on the belief that global warming is not reversible in the short run, science should explore issues from the perspective of homeland safety and security. To be protected, big corporations, banks and the capitalist elite call climatologists and geographers to design catastrophe simulation software that provides some information about where the next disaster will hit. In this vein, a new professional is rising, the economic-disaster-modeling geek. This expert seems to be more interested in finding and eliminating the risks to businesses, or finding ways to profit from such risks, than in protecting the environment. The philosophy of the science today is determined by the logic of digital screens. The simulation of a future that characterizes the digital world has replaced daily life (Virilio, 2010).

To what extent has science become an irreducible ally of the market? Not only the software, but also geologists today are poised to assist insurances companies, to know where nature will strike tomorrow. The problem of ecological risk seems not to be of extreme importance of experts, unless by the economic losses they generate. Modern science lacks critical discernment of the information it produces. More interested in anticipating the future than understanding the past, science, coupled to technology, simulates reality to mitigate risks. In this respect, Virilio and Baudrillard agree: "We might note a recent project whereby detection of major risks is reversed, since the computer in question is involved in producing said major risks. At the end of 2006, IBM effectively decided to build the most powerful super calculator in the world. To do so, it will use processors capable of up one million billon operations per second, accelerating by as much the reality of the disastrous progress in weapons of mass destructions ... which prompts personal question: after having resorted to meteorologists and other climatologists to calculate the economic risk of catastrophe, will the insurance and reinsurance companies one day have to call on the army and their new strategists to detect major ecological risk of nuclear proliferation" (Virilio 2010, p. 18).

Although the specialized literature to date has focused on the probabilistic nature of risk, it is socially negotiated and communicated. Skoll and Korstanje (2012) said that risks are conducive to economic production. To some extent, risks can be mitigated only once they have occurred, not before. If a correct decision is made on the basis of a scientific evaluation of risks, specialists admit the negative effects of disaster can be reversed. Rather, risks seem not to be a result of human's ignorance but of a gradual process that allowed the replication of capital. From the eighteenth century onwards, the dangers travellers face carrying goods from one to another point of the globe determines the final transaction price. From this viewpoint, risk was functional to the expansion of mercantilism and later capitalism. Each society develops particular forms of living democracy according to a sentiment of autonomy that alternates between efficiency and institutionalism. Given this argument, Skoll and Korstanje (2012) explain that risk works by the introduction of a text, a discourse, mediated, produced and defended by experts. While some properties may be widely exchanged, depreciating their value, others are banned but in high demand. The value of the latter's goods is so exorbitant that these goods become inalienable possessions. Furthermore, those actors who monopolize the possession of these taboo-goods enhance their prestige and gain further legitimacy than others. This generates an economic asymmetry among citizens. Validated by the future, ordinary people may buy for insurance-related protection prior to a disaster. As Baudrillard and Virilio put it, risks enable some tactics of capital reproduction based on the future. As a result, the present and history do not exist anymore. The disaster-related news leads people to mass consumption, while the nation-state introduces nationhood to legitimate the use of violence in case of internal dispute.

In her book *Unspeakable Violence*, Nicole Guidotti-Hernandez discusses the disciplinary instrument employed by states in borderlands to domesticate foreignness. They employ selective memory to reinforce the belief of nationhood awakening. Nation-states are formed under process of differentiation and its economic reorganization of territory. The centre of hegemony, like ideology, works by controlling what we denominate as authenticity. Mexico, for instance, promoted an image to the world based on the multiculturalism and respect for aborigines. However, less is said about how the government reserves the monopoly of force to discipline some peripheral ethnicities. Although the Aztec (*los indios*) heritage is elected to denote greatness, power and empire, other indigenous groups are relegated to secondary positions (Guidotti-Hernández, 2011). The guide books offered to international visitors not only trivialize their history, but also inflict an unspeakable violence to legitimate the cultural values of elites.

The events in Japan make one forget the causes and the effects of other catastrophes of the same magnitude such as that of Haiti, whose circumstances are similar, or of Chile, New Zealand or New Orleans. Culture fills the vacuum generated by modernity through which each actor and member of the group receives a value and identity which distinguishes them. Personal value is assigned to each citizen according to their salary. We connect this value to the person's capacity to be able to operate with risks, through professional advice. Thus, when we affirm that an accident impacts the market, we are not only harmed, but also we underestimate its internal logic. Accidents give value to the product. Natural or man-made disasters are valued in the market according to the specific demands of the consumer. It is not the same to travel to Ground Zero, where the Twin Towers were located, as to go to location X on the globe without media representation.

The importance of Baudrillard for disaster-related research has been ignored by some specialists, in part because few risk-related researchers are familiar with philosophical texts. Epistemologically speaking, Baudrillard was a pioneer who envisaged the connection between risk and the future by presenting an all-encompassing framework to understand the psychological impacts of disasters in our daily life. Baudrillard studies influenced the work of many other philosophers and sociologists interested in risk research such as Luhmann or Giddens.

Although risk perception studies use highly complex algorithmic mathematical categories, there is no fundamental epistemology to study risk from a qualitative perspective. Unfortunately for researchers in tourism who are interested in studying risk phenomenon and the threat of the natural disaster, these scholars do not publish their studies from the qualitative viewpoint. From projection techniques to diverse ethnographies or content analysis, there exists a never-ending variety of techniques that permit a scientific study of risk which escapes the logic of a number (Luhmann, 2006). According to Luhmann, one of the characteristics of risk is that despite being placed in a limited possibility of avoidance, it also becomes a product within the financial decision making process. An airplane crash, airline luggage theft (in the United States, usually perpetrated by US government security personnel), or a suicide bombing, among others provide choices of risk. Individuals assume their own risk when they participate in the decision making process that results in the expected, or not so expected, results. Events outside of the subject's decision-making process are understood as a threat or danger. This is one of the most common conceptual errors as applied to travel. Nonetheless, as we shall see in the following section, when the subject avoids the formal professional channels, risk increases.

## Administrative Council of the FCAJ (*Fundación Cultural*)

Argentino–Japonesa (Argentine–Japanese Cultural Foundation) headquartered in Buenos Aires' Japanese Garden (*Jardín Japonés*) organized a cultural trip to Japan to take place in 2012. The trip was organized prior to Japan's 2011 earthquake. The earthquake did not cancel the trip, but postponed it. However, the way in which it was organized changed considerably. This post disaster context travel engendered risks associated with radioactivity. Defying more than four decades of literature in risk-avoidance studies, what in normal circumstances would be a motive of rejection, here was the stepping-stone for travel.

The pamphlet or flier published by this association (FCAJ) mentions the number (quantification of the desire as an argument for sale) of questions that the association had received with respect to the potential trip: "A bit more than a month had passed since the terrible event in Japan, we gathered our forces to revisit the subject about the Cultural Trip to Japan to occur in 2012 and answered some of the questions. We received in those days a visit from the Ms. Srta. Mariko Hamamoto, a member of the Advisor Council of the Foundation's administration who currently was residing in Kyoto. She transmitted to us information about the current situation in Japan. With these concrete data, the FCAJ was able to evaluate the subject and decided to continue the trip."

Although the trip was planned prior to the earthquake, FCAJ could not avoid the fact that the situation had changed. The cultural trip to Japan was based on the ideal of brotherhood between communities, and as such this implied sharing of risks. The narrative of the trip to Japan, however, presents specifics that distinguish it from other narratives. The mediated image of the disaster, the virtual danger, the professional advice and the culture are current matters when we read the official letter of the FCAJ.

Likewise, it is of interest to note that the trip's tours had been scheduled to keep a considerable distance from the Fukushima nuclear plants. To the rapid recovery of Japan that the Argentines of Japanese descent longed for, is added the layout of an centerfold showing places to where they were making a pilgrimage. The trip literature implied that despite everything that had happened, the danger had not increased over that of other excursions the FCAJ had previously made to Japan. The organizers displayed a high degree of professionalism. For example, they informed the travelers that the trip would go through Canada rather than the United States to avoid visa issues, and were there to be any danger, the trip would then be cancelled. "The travel plan remains without modifications. For everyone's tranquility, we are informing you that the cities to be visited, according to our itinerary are some 500/600 kilometers to the south of where the tsunami struck and where the explosion at the Central Nuclear Electrical plant occurred (see details on map below). We are confident in a rapid Japanese recovery. We further want to inform you that our first meeting of about our Cultural Trip to Japan was a complete success, last Friday (March 4). We thank everyone who attended and we remind you of the topics to be discussed. ... Two possible itineraries have been handed out; these are the ones that the travel agencies with which we are working have given to us. Once the final group is formed the final itinerary will be developed. Although the majority of those interested are confident in that which has been proposed until now. With respect to the travel route, we will try to avoid the USA due to difficulties in obtaining visas. A possible route is through Canada. Getting a Canadian visa is a simple process. (Remember that these procedures are your responsibility) We calculate (including time on board, layovers) more than 30 hours of travel until we reach Japan. Once we have ten confirmed reservations the trip is confirmed."

A second aspect of tourism must be the cost-benefit analysis. The FCAJ, just as any organization that is sponsoring group travel, must weigh the trip's desired results, maximize earnings and minimize losses. Toward this end the FCAJ had to take into account security concerns, and assure the traveling public that they would be safe while demonstrating cognizance of the risks involved. Like Sontag's trip criticized by Baudrillard, there is nothing real in this travel. Tourists want to have an outstanding experience, already labeled by television. At a first glance, they seem to be risk-taking travelers, but in fact, the cultural adventure is completely safe. Commoditized, framed and sold before starting, this cultural travel may be equal to what Baudrillard calls a pseudo-event. The Baudrillard model is helpful in understanding that cultural consumption is related to the rational estimates of the outcomes. Travelers must evaluate the costs and benefits, emphasizing their own security. In such a process, culture becomes secondary in importance to security. Yet it is culture that is being consumed and cannot be overlooked. The FCAJ trip demonstrated that unfortunate incidents, the pain of others, and/or catastrophes in many cases do not break the logic of consumption. Instead, when combined with nationalism, they may add to its potential. In a hyper-reality risks are not real; they are configured by the media. Modern humans seek spectacle and the unique, but also seek a deepening of their cultural roots. We see this exemplified in the following from the FCAJ missive: "We look forward to your confirming that you will be on this spectacular Cultural Trip."

"Spectacle" has two possible semantic definitions. The first is connected to differences—that is, the trip is characterized not only by being in an area of supposed radioactive danger, but also by the unique Japanese traditions. Secondly, the abnormal situation in which the trip was undertaken is for many exceptional and this reinforces the need to maintain limits between a superordinate ego and the radicalization of the Other. In this context, the voyage can only be carried out if the members have all paid their fees, which indicates a subordination of the cultural with respect to the financial economic aspects. "We emphasize that this trip is organized by FCAJ, that it is NOT a tourism business. We count on the experience of more than 30 trips made by the Federation's president. Moreover, one of the members of the Foundation's Executive Council currently lives in Japan, and can guide us directly on subjects such as those mentioned at our meeting (Potters, important painters of sumi-e, kabuki theater, calligraphy, martial arts, government themes etc)."

Note that the professional advice given by the travel agent in the organization of tours has been relegated to being less important or not important at all. The organizers suggest that the trip to Japan will be carried out in a secure environment without an external organization. The FCAJ claims it has conducted some thirty trips to Japan, and has the assistance of one of its members who is a native of that country and who currently lives there. Through ostensibly shared knowledge and enhanced communication, the FCAJ has eliminated the necessity of a travel agent, and demonstrated assumed risk—as if it were an insurance company—without the need for professional advice.

The FCAJ literature implied that a tourism agency might detract from the seriousness of the cultural visit, and for this reason who better than the FCAJ to organize the voyage? As in this case and in other cases, the lack of professional advice in tourism, the decline of the travel agent, is present as a characteristic of the process of reliability on modernity and the individuation of risks as understood by Beck and Giddens. As professional advice declines, individual risks become greater. The experiences along with other fundamental aspects of professional advice are explained by the historic role that advisors have provided in the lives of people, from the ecclesiastic confessors to the therapists and travel agents. All of them have fulfilled a similar function: adding knowledge to the sense of possibility for civilization.

Reviewing the institutional letter, analyzed and sent by the FCAJ, permits us to understand the following elements:

a)  Modern travel and tourism is rooted in a financial-economic matrix which subordinates the social but does not eliminate it entirely.
b)  Travel needs a symbolic construction, a narrative sufficiently attractive and powerful to assure the travelers' interest. This criterion has varied throughout the centuries; however, in our age it is characterized by being anchored in the cultural, in tradition and in folklore.
c)  Indigeneity not only represents group cohesion, since it mentions the privilege of "being Japanese," but also prearranges a product ready for collective consumption. The culture absorbs the anguish of the unknown by means of building risk.
d)  For the exposed, the danger or the potential danger that the Japanese earthquake represented and the ensuing difficulties in that country to deal with its problems in its radioactive plants play an ambiguous role. On one hand, they attract a Japanese public disturbed by the tragedy, while on the other hand, they alienate certain spaces that are now out of bounds. The tour is possible thanks to this combination of attraction and contained danger.

It is not hard to see in moments of emergencies and/or natural disasters, that diverse mechanisms come forth that help groups to understand what is happening to avoid group disintegration. As explained by Baudrillard, nationalism and the proclivity for consumer culture are the social mechanisms whose function lies in sense of world events. Tragedy supposes a radical extermination, but at the same time individual and group strength to overcome the same. In this context national pride is demonstrated soon after an event like an earthquake or tsunami. What we find in play is the necessity of making sense of something that appears to make no sense. The missive's message was simply stating that yes, a great part of Japan has been destroyed with a high cost in human life and materials, but the survivors realize that despite all the community is still standing.

## Conclusion

After review, we consider that Baudrillard's texts would be of importance for the risk-related research in next decades. They allude to a fertile ground to study the connection between cultural entertainment, media and nationalism. Further, Baudrillard reminds us that the strengthening of the group for reconstruction and the role of nationalism are important at the time of confronting reality. In that instant are when the national and the traditional converge; the market is the entity capable of organizing individual passions and sublimating them into established institutions (Baudrillard, 1995a; 1995b). The letter issued by FCAJ shows any travel, even the cultural, is part of an economical matrix, which delineates the boundaries between safe and unsafe geography. Experts and specialists, in this case the tour operators, suggest to travelers the best options for achieving a unique experience, but this does not mean such an experience is real. The national-being represents an attraction for travels as a type of brotherhood, which is not altered even by spatial distance. Being Japanese is a reason for pride, because after the quake, Japan is still working to recover the obliterated industries, schools and households. The claim alludes to a sentiment of ethnocentrism. Following the explanation of Lasch, this process of victimization is narcissistic, closed to the dialogue with others. As a result of this temporal blindness, in which the real causes of the Fukushima tragedy are not discussed, they will provide a fertile source for the next disaster.

The concept of "hyper-reality," a term coined by Baudrillard, is of paramount importance to expand the current understanding of how any disaster leads to the next. This construct is conductive for the elite to introduce radical changes that otherwise would be rejected by public opinion. After a catastrophe, capitalism offers higher and newly recycled buildings, taller skyscrapers, further modern infrastructures, faster mobile technologies, and so on. The important aspect that lies below the surface in these processes is the need to create future order out of chaos. The market recreates new fictions by which the possibility of new disasters may be borne. In this context, a disaster can be transformed into a symbolic mediator and product of consumption giving rise to what tourism specialists call "dark tourism." Modern society not only sells tranquility and security to its consumers, but also through crisis management gives birth to new products. Tourism, culture and the travel industry are part of the never ending cycle of creation that perhaps first started with the Big Bang. Thus, we are in the presence of the end of disasters as events structured that provide social meaning. Today, catastrophes are socially and journalistically enshrined in the world of consumerism. After all, what nobody discusses is, as Voltaire said, earthquakes do not kill people, buildings do ... disasters are human inventions, produced by human intervention into environment.

# 4 Thana-Capitalism

"In practice, the new society operated not by the wholesale destruction of all that had inherited from the old society, but by selectively adapting the heritage of the past to its own use. There is no sociological puzzle about the readiness of bourgeois society to introduce a radical individualism in economics ... and to tear up all traditional social relations in the process" (Hobsbawm, 1994, p. 16)

## Introduction

The multiplication of risks which oscillates from terrorism to virus outbreaks or natural disasters defies today the conceptual framework of the welfare state. Whether our grandparents endowed politicians with their trust, to be protectors of community, these days they are portrayed as liars, professional swindlers or inefficient autocratic staff who are insensible to what people feel (Sunstein, 2002a; Biocca, 2005). Although disasters were inherited to social imaginaries and cultural consumptions, for example, expressed in movies as *Volcano, Deep Impact* or *The Perfect Storm* among others, in this new century fiction becomes in part of reality (Quarantelli, 1960; 2006; Brunsma & Picou, 2008). The shocking attack to WTC in New York known as the financial centre of the World inaugurated a new age of fear and uncertainness where West understood that nobody was safer anymore and in any place. It is tempting to say that risk studies and texts on risk perception flourished in almost all disciplines from engineering to social sciences (Skoll, 2010; Korstanje, 2015); in this vein, many philosophers focused on the problem of risk as an ethical quandary resulted from the decline of trust accelerated by late-capitalism (Beck, 2002; Sennett, 2011). From Baudrillard to Bauman or Soyinka, these writers devoted considerable attention to analyzing the effects of fear in daily life. In terms of Baudrillard, a new spectacle of disaster, which is forecasted and disseminated by the media for entertainment, enlarges a much deeper dissociation between reality and fiction (Kellner, 2005). At some extent, albeit these studies shed light on a new time which was next to come, less attention was paid to some aspects that explain further on why this happens. This conceptual discussion not only continues with earlier efforts in risk studies, but also coins the term "thana-capitalism" to refer this uncanny fascination for disaster-related landscapes. What the doctrine of risk-zero was unable to explain was the reasons why technological advance did not suffice to make a safer world. Following the rational paradigm, external or internal threats can be found by the net of experts who work for state. Whenever these risks are located, experts should intervene according to protocols of surveillance. In this process science would play a crucial role expanding the produced knowledge in order for society to be protected (Beck, 1992). If Harvey (1989) indicated that oil embargo was the epicenter that started postmodernism, and Paul Virilio (2010) evinced the rise of uncertainness that subordinated the security of the workforce to profits and businesses, the evolution and consolidation of a "culture of fear" remained unchecked. In this chapter we hold the thesis that disasters do not affect cultures; rather, cultures are predetermined by earlier disasters or traumatic events. Interesting evidence can be found in founding myths such as that of Noah, where God dispenses an apocalyptic natural disaster for the reconstruction of a new exemplary culture. At a first look, Noah is the first survivor and the only chosen by God to continue with humankind on the earth. Doubtless, the force and influence of this myth in a capitalist system is stronger than in other cultures, simply because it paves the ways for the configuration of a sentiment of exemption, in which the destruction of all is based in the salvation of a few. Ideologically speaking, Noah's story leads to a process of social Darwinism, in which case capitalism was successfully reproduced worldwide. This reflects an asymmetrical system where a privileged group amasses almost 80% of produced wealth while the rest are pressed to live with limited resources. As the backdrop, the culture of disaster within modern capitalism aims at disorganizing social ties. In so doing, the derived narcissism is adopted as the main cultural value of society. The question whether capitalism expanded faster than analysts precluded correspond with two key factors: *the need to be different* and *the need for protection*. The society of risk sets the pace to a new capitalism (thana-capitalism), where the presence of death allows changes that otherwise would not be feasible. In these days of thana-capitalism, life is seen as a long race where only one will be the winner. The death of Others which is present in newspapers, television and the Internet not only makes us feel special because we are in a race after all, but also reminds us of how special we are. This is the reason why disasters captivate today's global audience. At the time, they exhibit the disgrace in Others news reinforce the supremacy of West over other cultures. Secondly, leisure practices such as classic "Sun and Sea" tourism are changed to new forms where mass disaster or mourning spaces are the main attraction. This new segment, known by some specialists as thana-tourism or dark tourism, recycles spaces of disasters or mass death to be visually commoditized to international consumers who need to be close to an Other's death. If older leisure practices embraced an apollonian view of beautiness that invited workers to spend time and money in paradise-alike destinations, now we are witness of the rise of a new class, death-seekers. What would be more than interesting to discuss is the intersection of death and consumption. It signals to radical shifts that certainly denote the beginning of a new capitalism, thana-capitalism.

## Thanaptosis

Originally, the term was coined by William Cullen Bryant (1948) to describe a state of nostalgia to see life through the eyes of death. It signalled the need to recycle life through death and vice versa. In other terms, we are not born to live, because we are dying while growing. This neologism comes from the Greek word *thanatos*, which means death.

In the psychological fields, one of the pioneers to discover the force of Thanatos to sublimate our desires was Sigmund Freud. Across over the psychological structure of individuals, two inborn drives coexist: life and death drives (as Norse culture). The death drive can be understood as a bodily instinct to return to a state earlier than our birth. Whereas Eros was orientated to protect life through sexual energy, Thanatos appealed to (self) destruction (Freud, 1920).

In this token, modernity and death seem to be inextricably intertwined. In this vein, Ariès calls the attention to the fact that in the Middle Ages, peasants were subject to countless dangers and real death was just around the corner. With the expansion of life expectancy, modern citizens expanded their hopes to live but undomesticated death, producing a paradoxical situation. Effects of disaster or mass death will resonate in modern capitalist society higher than in medieval times (Ariès, 2013). In a world full of social inequalities, not surprisingly, death corresponds with a criterion of exclusion but what is more important; in the current times, death-seekers not only are moved by Thanatos or a death-drive, but are in quest of reinforcing their ego by the Other's death. Only in this way they feel unique, exceptional or beyond the law. These cultural values which are new for many social scientists, has revolutionized the already existent notion of beautiness. As Auge put it, travellers over past centuries were captivated by the reading of novels which engaged the reader with the next trip. The role of imagination was a powerful instrument to imagine "the Other," whereas modern tourism was introduced to neglect and subordinate the position of the Others. In consequence, laypeople do not make the decision to travel elsewhere; rather, the image of travels at dream destinations is imposed on consumers (Auge, 1997). Nonetheless, the world described by Auge is pretty different than this. Those landscapes, which some time ago, inspired poems, writers and poets set the pace to the advance of news, or TV programs that tell us how "Others" die, or zones effaced by natural disasters. This is one of others indicators that evinces we are inevitably passing from risk capitalism to thana-capitalism. To understand the reason of their own life, death-seekers (within thana-capitalism) need to experience death through the eyes of "Others." To put this in bluntly, modern citizens need to gaze how others die in order to have a meaningful live. In medieval age, peasants were physically constricted to move freely but their imagination took often them to places where others cannot easily go. Religion and the belief in a better world hereafter configured a social ethos that makes medieval man happier. In modern times, mobilities played a vital role expanding the boundaries where geographically a citizen may travel but its imagination declined to a small-world. In a realm, where God has died, the consciousness resists to die accepting, in the terms of Riesman, an Other-directed view of life (Korstanje, 2015). In his classic work *The Lonely Crowd* Riesman was the first to note economy and social organization are inevitably inter-linked. The good-exchange delineates the cultural institutions to forge a common "character. In ancient times, tradition-directed character imposed an economy of subsistence, where tradition and lore played important positions as organizers of social life. With some economic changes brought by mercantilism, the tradition-oriented trait set the pace to a new one, inner-directed development. In times of reform, puritanism appealed to the law-abiding and self-conforming. After WWII, American society experienced the change to "other directedness" where people are in quest of events that occur beyond their immediate scopes. This other-directed personality, not only allowed a state of exchange and wealth accumulation but also paved the ways for the advent of globalization. The interests for others which can be expressed in modern tourism or even in journalism are a direct effect of this trait. The problem of a society attached to spectacle was originally addressed by Guy Debord in 1967, in his masterful work *The Society of Spectacle*. Following Debord, one might realize that daily life is being degraded by the imposition of representations, stereotypes, and images to the extent that "the being" embraces merely appearing instead of other values. As commodities, micro-social relations are emptied according to representational landscapes that are dramatically exposed. Unless otherwise reversed, the society of spectacle irremediably will usher humankind into an atmosphere of inauthenticity and fetishism (Debord, 2012).

## Dark Tourism: Obsessing with Death

As discussed in earlier section, dark tourism became in one of the most growing segments of tourism in recent days. Zone of extreme poverty situated in the periphery as India, Brazil, or South-Africa offers a fertile ground for visiting places characterized by slumming and ghettoization. Similarly to dark tourism, slum tourism initiated new trends where the criterion of attraction seems to be *human suffering* (Freire-Medeiros, 2014; Reijinders, 2009; Tzanelli, 2015a,b; 2016). In fact, as Tzanelli (2016) puts it, thana-tourism and slum-tourism are inextricably intertwined since both are efforts to re-interpret the pastime according to the needs of financial elite, which do not make responsible for the arbitrariness of colonization process. The aura of special travellers, very important persons dotted of higher mobility is reinforced to gaze "others had not the same luck." It is interesting to discuss to what extent capitalism, even in these modern times, encouraged the mobilities of few, constrained the workforce to immobility. Quite aside from this initial debate, scholars interested in dark tourism issues agree that visitors are aimed at experiencing new sensation, or are in quest of novel experiences, where the "death of Others" serves to shed light on their own lives (Bowman & Pezzulo, 2009; Buda & McIntosh, 2013; Cohen, 2011; Lennon & Foley, 2000; Seaton 1996; Strange & Kempa, 2003; Stone, 2006; 2011; Stone & Sharpley, 2008). In this respect, Seaton defines thana-tourism as the travel dimension toward thanaptosis understood this as a trip to a site wholly or partially motivated by the desire of meeting death (Seaton, 1996).

Other of the authorative voices in this theme, Stone confirms that dark tourism represents an attempt of imaging own death before death takes place. Dark tourists not only are interested in human suffering, they also want to understand their lives in context of the Other's pain. Far from being sadist consumers, as critical voices preclude, Stone adheres to the thesis that dark tourism represents an anthropological need to anticipate the own death by means of Others' death (Stone, 2012). Rather, Erik Cohen (2011) dangled the possibility that dark tourism works as a mechanism of education so that the next generations learn further about those events that caused great trauma to society. In view of that, Cohen divides *in populo site*, which signaled to those sites where disaster took hit, from, *re-created sites* more oriented to exploit profits from a sad event. The concept of authenticity delineates the borders of visitor's experience to the extent to generate different types of reactions. For Cohen, dark tourism epitomizes an instrument which very well can be used for educative purposes.

An interesting doctoral dissertation authored by Stephanie Yuill (2004) held the thesis that the fascination of death and disasters can be framed in profiles to expand the current understanding of the issue. Most death-site visitors not only look for new sensations but also have many questions regarding some historical aspects of tragedies. Far from morbidity, educational aims and the quest of heritage are the two main motivations these tourists follow. Tony Walter (2009) found a correlation between dark tourism and media attention to these types of sad events. Since the law is the institution that links dead with living no less true is that disasters some agents are invested to gather information and explain why this happens. In aboriginal cultures this role is played by religious leaders and shamans, while in modern societies it was reserved for social scientists and journalists. For Walter, once society was pacified, for example comparing with medieval feuds, dark tourism sites are the only way people have to mediate with death. Rojek suggests on the importance of social background in the configuration of identities which are embedded with dark-site consuming (Rojek, 1997). In his project *Writing the Dark Side of Travel*, Johnathan Skinner (2012) adheres to the belief that tourists who visit spaces of disasters or black-spots are emotionally moved to understand their own lives. All those who witnessed these spectacles like hearing a lesson of human suffering or about event which escaped from the threshold of human control. Far from being a mere fetish, Skinner adds, one of the limitations of dark tourism sites lies in the fact while some voices are over-valorized others are silenced.

As the previous backdrop, Sather-Wagstaff (2011) adamantly examined Ground Zero, a crater left where Twin Towers in New York were. Not only did this event caused a great shock for Americans, but also it created a great mourning for families and relatives of victims. Doubtless, in Sather-Wagstaff's account, this represents a real site of dark tourism. Throughout a self-ethnography she found that dark tourism is used to mediate between self and its conception of future. This happens simply because we are familiar with the irreversibility of death, and struggle to stop it; our desires to live appears as a powerful reason to exorcise death. As expression of the solidarity, dark tourism makes us emotionally closer to Others' suffering.

However, from Pearl Harbor to Hiroshima, these sites are commoditized to tell part of the true, whenever politicians take direct intervention. Unlike other scholars, she considers dark tourism pitted against heritage. To overcome the ethnocentric view of heritage given by political tergiversation, dark tourism provides with an opportunity to channel emotions in order for the community to understand the reasons of disaster.

With some exceptions, one of the conceptual problems of applied research or fieldwork in dark tourism issues not only is the lack of shared meaning of the term, but also an "over-reliance" in positivism which postulates the asking is the only way toward truth. As my own experience as ethnologist, I have a plenty of anecdotes where interviewees simply lie or are not familiar with their inner emotions. Under some contexts, administering closed-or-open questionaries or intrusive interviews obscures more than it clarifies. This is the reason to reconsider dark tourism beyond what tourists or visitors believe. Apparently, they will respond their motivations are associated to heritage consumption, or knowing further on tragic event enrooted in history, but far from this, their motivations go to the opposite direction (Korstanje, 2014a). Therefore, in earlier approaches Korstanje (2011; 2014b), Korstanje and Ivanov (2012) and Korstanje and George (2015) exerted a radical criticism on dark-tourism approaches. Underpinned in the propositions of Malinowski that death causes a symbolic rupture of in-group members and officialdom, a gap which should be fulfilled by rituals, Korstanje argues convincingly that disasters not only produces a great trauma in society, but rattles her sociopolitical scaffolding. At some extent, tourism broadly speaking and dark tourism more specifically, work as mechanisms of resilience to give a lesson to community about the event (Korstanje, 2014a; Korstanje & Ivanov, 2012). This discourse facilitates the steps toward an efficient recovery process. Nonetheless, over recent years, a radical shift surfaced (Korstanje & George, 2015). To wit, disasters pose as the commodity for media and cultural industries to construct a "spectacle" that instills a combination of fear and entertainment to a much wider globalized audience (Baudrillard, 1997; 2003; Jameson, 2002). In this respect, Naomi Klein (2007) explores the obsession for capitalism to produce allegories of disasters through the media. She contends that the elite allude to fear not only for the workforce to accept policies that otherwise should be rejected, but also to recycle geographical spaces according to Schumpeter's term, the logic of "the creative destruction." As I have (2014b; 2015) observed, in post-disaster contexts, victims face a great mourning or extreme loss, which disorganizes their feelings. However, they feel that after all, gods have protected them. Despite the great obliteration, survivors develop a biased image of themselves, understanding they have survived by some supernatural strongholds such as virtue, force or any type of superior spirit. Just as "Others" have been doomed, survivors were chosen by God(s), fate or destiny. In view of this, these chosen ones follow a goal, which often is associated with violence resistance or the quest for justice. Reactions like this are typical of victims in a post-trauma condition, but if it is not regulated, pathological forms of behaviors as nationalism, chauvinism or disproportionate ethnocentrism can emerge. The idea of exceptionalism whereby survivors sublimate their pain leads toward *a state of narcissism*, where they feel special, superior, more civilized and outstanding with respect to Others (Korstanje, 2015). Precisely, this is the moot point that characterizes the ideological core of thana-capitalism, where the need to gaze at disasters and victimization coexist. To put this brutally, this is a society that highlights death over other social values. In next section, the passage from risk-capitalism to a thana-capitalism will be placed under the critical lens of scrutiny.

## The Risk Society

The society of risk, technically, starts with the nuclear accident in Chernobyl, Ukraine. This event reorganized the already existent hierarchal order to a new reflective logic. In decline, the classic institutions created by welfare state were unable to protect citizens no longer. Ulrich Beck, who was one of the pioneers in envisaging a radical change in political making up, argued that the sense of community is now based on the risk perception (Beck, 1992). In the society of risks, the process of knowledge production leads to a state of complexity that creates a paradoxical situation. The same technology originally designed to make safer the lives of people, if unregulated can result in a real disaster. The old world of classes where the first Marxists exerted their radical critique has set the pace to a new one. The classic division between the rich and the poor, or the haves and the have-nots, has gone forever. Now, all citizens seem to be equally at risk. The stage of globalization that accelerated the transport orchestrated a closed system which is very well market-oriented to mass consumption. However, the production of risks seems to be inverse proportional to the current distribution of wealth. This suggests that concepts as wealth, democracy, or equality will be replaced by security, risk, protection and so forth. At some extent, capitalism showed a lack of permeability with environment which may usher the Occident into an ending collapse (Beck, 1992). In this respect, another senior sociologist, Giddens, adheres to Beck that the process of reflexibility institutionalized a culture of risk, or "radical doubt" altering the ontological security of lay-peoples. Based on attachment theory, Giddens acknowledges that social trust works as a protective cocoon, which is given by caretakers to children in early stages of development. Any potential failure that undermines social trust will result in serious doubts in a child's adulthood. The same applies for modern society, since modernity undermines certainness in some parameters of daily life, while adopting high levels of risk. The successive enhancements in the knowledge-based technology make society more vulnerable because the decision-making process paradoxically reproduces new risks.

> "The reorganization of daily life through abstract systems creates many routines forms of activity having a higher level of predictability than most contexts in pre-modern cultures. Through the protective cocoon, most people are buffered most of the time from the experience of radical doubt as a serious challenge either to the routines of daily activity or to more

far-reaching ambitions. The dilemma of authority vs doubt is ordinarily resolved through a mixture of routine and commitment to a certain form of lifestyle, plus the vesting of trust in a given series of abstract systems." (Giddens, 1991, p. 196)

Although Beck, Giddens and their followers deserve recognition by identifying not only that institutions were mutating but also that risk posed as a mediator between citizens and their institutions, no less true is that capitalism is far from proposing a world where all citizens would be equal. In fact, the gap between have and have-nots has been enlarged. In the United States, the GINI coefficient, which is often used by economists to measure inequalities, has grown from 0.361 in 1969 to 0.865 in 2009 (Babones, 2012). In this respect, Niklas Luhmann adheres to the thesis that risk and threats are not the same phenomenon. While risks are enrooted in the principle of "contingency," which means that the decision-maker has the possibility to avoid its immediate effects, dangers or threats are externally imposed on the subject. The precautionary platform, where Beck and Giddens are adjoined, misjudges this by endowing the working classes with responsibilities for events that are produced beyond their control. Luhmann adds, the groups that make decisions never face the risks. To set an example, airplane accidents are threats not only for passengers but also for the owner, who had the direct intervention of costs and materials (Luhmann, 1990). With the same in mind, other voices such as Klein advocated the thesis that risk society is allegorically constructed to protect the interests of financial elites (Klein, 2007). Philosopher Zygmunt Bauman explains convincingly that "in the liquid society of consumers," society only reacts for those events which have economic effects. Since Marx's times, things have changed a lot. Nowadays, workers are commoditized to struggle with others in the marketplace, to be sold or desired by others. The gaze of Others, as it was formulated by Riesman (1953), Urry (2002), Tzanelli (2015a; 2016) or Hannam and Know (2005), was of paramount importance in the configuration of a consuming society. It is interesting not to lose sight that surveillance-related technology marks a criterion of status and distinction for those who can pay for that. The process of securitization empowered by capitalist-owners not only violates the workforce, but also draws an exemplary center where laypeople cannot enter, as demonstrated by buying insurance, or adopting high-tech means as a sign of status for the chosen citizens while the problem of crime remains unresolved (Bauman, 2013; Bauman & Lyon, 2013). Bauman acknowledges the divide-and-rule logic produces imbalances within the system. These inequalities open the door for the imposition of competence as a sign of distinction.

In his recent book *A Difficult World* (Korstanje, 2015), I observed that capitalism should not be seen as the best of all possible worlds, but was indeed success in expanding worldwide. This occurred in view of two combined aspects. At a closer look, capitalism is centered on what Hofstadter dubbed "social Darwinism," a biological doctrine adapted to proclaim the supremacy of White race over others, and even the Anglo-Saxons over other cultures. As Darwin noted species adapt to environment to survive. Those who evince the better skills for this adaptation will rule over others who will perish (the survival of the fittest). Replicated this theory to social world, Galton (Darwin's nephew) in England and Graham Sumner in US proposed an innovative model. With the help of medical discourse which proclaimed the supremacy of English races over others ethnicities, social Darwinists believed that those human groups whose strongholds have consolidated in their adaptation to environment have more probabilities to reach wealthier conditions than other races. Anglo-Saxons were ethnically and culturally superior to other groups since they evolved in more success economic organizations. The theory based on the survival of the fittest was replaced by *"the survival of strongest."* The second element manipulated by capital-owners is risk. Even Beck only says a partial truth at time of describing risk society. The fact is that richer classes dangled the probabilities to buy further protection than more vulnerable lower classes. In this way, one might speculate that risk-society produces serious economic imbalances in workers who are endorsed to manage the external risks on their own. In recent times, however, a new type of capitalism up-surged: thana-capitalism. What are the main commonalities and difference of thana-capitalism and risk society?

For exegetes of thana-capitalism, who echo social Darwinists, economic inequalities among class can be compared to the conception of life. If millions spermatozoids compete for the fecundation of an ovule, this suggests that only one will be the winner. Unlike risk society, in this new age, the few have concentrated wealth while the rest live with fewer resources.

The *society of risk* operates under the logic of protection. No matter neither the causes nor the ideological position, nation-state endorses the market to function as protector of citizenry. The means of production corresponds with a decentralized way, where the process of reflexibility plays a crucial role. This leads to the atomization of agents, which are segmented by marketing experts to be bombarded by different products. In this epoch that begins with Chernobyl, society changes from an economy of producers to an economy of consumers (Donohue, 2003). The paradigm of protection supports the over-valorization of Science as the only instrument capable to provide and disseminate valuable information to make the life safer. Undoubtedly, Chernobyl poses a serious dilemma to the use of technology. The same took-kit used to protect society can be fertile toward a real disaster. Paul Virilio has envisaged this apocalyptic scenario in his book *The University of Disaster*. He claims that science played a role subordinated to main business corporations, which are more interested in enhancing their profits than in preventing disasters. The days of science as an instrument toward a better world have passed. The greatest business corporations appeal to science not only to predict the weather, by the use of many climate catastrophe simulation software, but in introducing "an economic disaster modelling-geek." The nexus of experts seem to be more interested in locating and eliminating all risks that may threaten the current means of production, than in helping others (Virilio, 2010). In this world, which has gone, risk, risk perception and the industry of insurances have pivoted the interactions in the societal order.

## The Roots of Thana-Capitalism

The epicenter of thana-capitalism comes from the attacks to World Trade Center perpetrated by Al-Qaeda on 11 September of 2001. This shocking blow represented a turning point where Islam radicalism showed not only the weaknesses of West, but also how the means of transport, which were a badge of pride in the United States, were employed as mortal weapons directed toward civil targets. Educated and trained in the best Western universities, jihadists showed the dark side of the society of mass consumption. Many of the steps followed by Al-Qaeda were emulated from a management guidebook. This man-made disaster showed the proud United States of America that regardless of strength, power or levels of development of the country, terrorism will be present in all central nations. From this moment on, nobody will feel safe at any time and in any place. As the Catholic Church demonstrated in Lisbon's earthquake of 1755, the rational basis of risk experts or risk-related analysis was placed under the critical lens of scrutiny. Beyond what radical conservatives in Bush's administration precluded, this event initiated a new age where the concept of security and prevention start to dilute.

All these discussed indicators set the path to a more complex scenario, where economy turns chaotic (unpredictable after financial stock and market crisis in 2008) where the atomized demands become in a competence of all against all (in Hobbesian terms). The Darwinist allegory of the survival of strongest can be found as the main culture value of thana-capitalism in a way that is captivated by cultural entertainment industries and cinema. Films such as *The Hunger Games* portray an apocalyptic future where the elite govern with iron rule different colonies. A wealthy capitol which is geographically situated in Rocky Mountain serves as an exemplary center, a hot-spot of consumption and hedonism where the spectacle prevails. The oppressed colonies are rushed to send their warriors who will struggle with others to death, in a bloody game that keeps people exciting. Although all participants work hard to enhance their skills, only one will reach the glory. The same can be observed in reality shows such as *Big Brother*, where participants neglect the probabilities to fail simply because they over-valorize their own strongholds. This exactly seems to be what engages citizens to compete with others to survive, to show "they are worth of survive." In sum, the *sentiment of exceptionality* triggered by these types of ideological spectacles disorganizes the social trust.

Last but not least, capitalism signals to the constructions of allegories containing death prompting a radical rupture of self with others. Whenever we see ourselves as special, put others of different condition asunder. In a context of turbulences, the imposition of these discourses is conducive to the weakening of social fabric. Thematizing disasters by dark-tourism consumption patterns, entails higher costs the disaster repeats in a near future. The political intervention in these sites covers the real reasons behind the event, which are radically altered to protect the interests of status quo. The political and economic powers erect monuments to symbolize sudden mass death or trauma-spaces so that society reminds a lesson, which allegory contains a biased or galvanized explanation of what happened.

Though at some extent, community needs to produces these allegories to be kept in warning, the likelihood that the same disaster hits again seems to be a question of time (Korstanje, 2014b).

As the previous argument given, thana-capitalism offers death (of others) as a spectacle not only revitalizes the daily frustrations, but enhances a harmed ego. Visiting spaces of disasters during holidays, or watching news on terrorist attacks at home, all represents part of the same issue: *the advent of a new class of death-seekers.*

As fieldworker I have developed a psychological profile after visiting several spaces of dark tourism in the third and first worlds. At some extent, far from being a naïve activity, tourism exhibits the main values of society and her economic production. Therefore, observing closer how the patterns of holiday-makers as well as leisure practices evolved is a valid lens to understand much deeper social changes. Detractors of industrialism, as Hofstadter, ignite the discussion around social Darwinism. We are playing a game, which has fewer probabilities of success. In thana-capitalism we felt happy for the Other's failure. The competition fostered by the ideology of capitalism offers the salvation for few ones, at the expense of the rest. To realize the dream of joining the "selected people," we accept the Darwinist rules. Whenever one of our direct competitors fails, we feel an insane happiness. I argue that a similar mechanism is activated during our visit to dark tourism sites: we do not strive to understand, we are just happy because we escaped death and have more chances to win the game of life.

As adamantly and incessantly discussed throughout this book, the unpleasant sensation of reading newspapers is compensated by the happiness the self develops through the other's suffering –a rite necessary to avoid or think about one's own potential pain. Starting from the premise that the self is morally obliged to assist the other to reinforce a sentiment of superiority, avoidance preserves the ethical base of social relationships (Mead, 2009). Nonetheless, this in-born drive has been manipulated beyond the limits of a reasonable narcissism. Originally, Slavoj Žižek agrees that Christianity needs from to pose a message of self-destruction which is emulated by Christ to become God. In the core of Christendom is enrooted a lesson that encourages the betrayal as a guiding value (Žižek, 2003).

Capitalism has expanded by the introduction of social Darwinism where the struggle of all against all prevents the social coordination and conflict. To legitimize this, ideological stories serves as a disciplinary mechanisms of control. This seems to be exactly what we have discussed respecting Noah's Ark, or games such as on the reality show *Big Brother*.

## Conclusion

To cut a long story short, thana-capitalism alludes to what Baudrillard dubbed as "the spectacle of disaster," as the main criterion of attraction. Disasters provides to thana-capitalism with the commodity to disorganize the social ties among workers in order to introduce an atmosphere of social Darwinism where all competes with all to survive. This can be observed not only in cultural entertainment industries but also in other institutions as well, as a new trend in tourism to visit spaces of mass death and mourning. Far from pursuing educational aims, rather, these sites are aesthetically designed to make feel visitors they are special. In a secular society where gods have gone forever, life is imagined as a long race where only a few are mythically empowered to win. The death of others represents a new opportunity to feel one is still in the race. This confers an aura of superiority that leads individuals to narcissism. As a result of this, mistrust paves the ways for the social tie decline. The psychological effects of dark tourism, disaster-cinema, Newspapers covering tragic events, local crime or even programs such as *Assassination Discovery* or *Criminal Minds* are not very different from what a survivor experiences in post-traumatic contexts. As explained, survivors (in the case of cinema watchers) feel that after all, gods have protected them. It triggers a necessary sentiment of narcissism that helps to the process of resilience. Survivors understand that they gained superpowers which saved their lives. Unless emotions of these natures not to controlled, it may very well disorganize the existent social bondage because people start to develop a "pathological state of narcissism," where the so-called *chosen people* keep the right to interact with others primus inter-pares. This is exactly the manner how *thana-capitalism* works that explains our obsessions for disasters, and other's death. If the sense of protection marked the pace in the society of risk, now witnessing the Other's death (even thana-tourism) posed as the main cultural value of thana-capitalism. In next chapter, we will discuss the roots of evilness as the platform for what humans feel the world is unjust with them. Not only disasters, but other calamities are fertile ground for a much deeper process of victimization which leads peoples toward thana-capitalism.

# 5    Understanding the Origin of Evilness

## Introduction

Christendom has evolved over centuries based on the legend of an Arch-Angel who embraced evilness, Lucifer. This figure garnered the attention of philosophers and theologians. At a closer look, one of the main conceptual doubts, questions and dilemmas Lucifer wakes up associates to the nature of evil. Starting from the premise that an all-powerful God created an angel who will become in a monstrosity later, it opens a question respecting to the credibility of goodness. Although, the existence of God was adamantly discussed in Catholic circles (Bernstein, 2006), the philosophical problem of evil remains unchecked. While for some voices, Lucifer falls showing the unconditional love of God (testing the roots of theodicy), for others, this represents the evidence of his inexistence. There is no redemption, following this axiom, without sin and forgiveness. Conducive to lead humankind toward the Lord, Lucifer plays the role of devil's advocate tempting to those he was designed to protect. Anthropologists and historians devoted considerable resources in understanding Lucifer enrooted in the archetype of medieval princes who often defied or conspired Kings to enhance more influence and power. As an example of what happens with deviant princes, Lucifer during years was conducive to the authority of Catholic Church and nobility in the Middle Ages (Muchembled, 2000; Russell, 1977; 1986). For Jean Markale (2006) evilness embodies problems for the status quo to control deviance. Therefore, Lucifer is not very different than other antiheroes such as Prometheus, or Gilgamesh. They are catalysts cultures construct to blame whenever things do not come out as planned.

A separate chapter is needed regarding the role played by witchcraft and its effects on the inheritance system. Interesting studies showed the intersection of economy and witchcraft to the extent to suggest the concept of evilness served as a disciplinary discourse to control "women" (Ezzy, 2006; Kohnert, 1996; Middleton, 1967; Pfau, 2013; Wilby, 2013), but unfortunately little attention was given to Lucifer as the "Prince of darkness." Beyond the inspiration of panic instilled by Lucifer, first and foremost after the film *The Exorcist*, we need to understand this issue as a mythical anti-hero embedded with Abrahamic mythologies. Discursively Lucifer is unreal unless in our system of myths. Therefore, this section combines the contribution of anthropology in the examination of myths, with content analysis. In this discussion, we hold the thesis that Lucifer represents an old fear to the death of the Son, a belief which conjoined emotionally with one of the discourses of thana-capitalism: bio-technology and fertility.

## Mythology

While the whole creation moves in this earth by inborn drives, humans are the only ones who prefigure their own death (Gebauer & Wulf, 2009). As myth-producers, we are living and dwelling in this world, reminding us of not only our importance with respect to animals but also our sacred connectedness to gods (Castoriadis, 2006). At some extent, religion may be considered as good platform to resolve the problem of time, life and death. British anthropologist Evans-Pritchard (1977) acknowledged the significance of myth to legitimize the customs and social structure. Unconsciously, daily practices are culturally determined by the manners of gods and heroes transmitted from generation to generation in mythical stories. Whether myths are defined as abstract construes operating in a type of myth-text, rites are studied from the fieldwork. Methodogically, ethnographers reached consensus in confirming rituals and myths not only change from organization to organization but vary across time (Leach, 1954; 1965; Morris, 1995). In fact, Malinowski, one of the fathers of modern anthropology, understood myths as guiding narrative that often confer to people understanding about their world. As founding parents overcome the obstacles in past, in the same way, we have to move in these days. Without exception, humans are myth-producers, and there is no culture insensitive to the influence of myths (Malinowski, 1998). As Claude Lévi-Strauss (1991; 1995; 2002; 2003) puts it, the production of myths is used to understand the contradictions of life. At the time we are born, we are dying. Why should we live if some later day we will come across our death?

Doubtless, Mircea Eliade was one of the leading voices in leaving an all-encompassing model to explore myths. Per his stance, myths should be understood as "sacred stories," which describe nonhistorical events where heroes challenged the temple of gods, or suffered great tribulations to protect humankind. Based on the idea Lévi Strauss was wrong, Eliade confirms that myths endorse legitimacy to the connection of parents and their offspring. In this vein, Silverstein argues convincingly that death presses the self to connect with its inner-life. The coexistence with "Others" depends on the ability of religion to instill a belief in life hereafter. The Other's death exhibits not only our limited nature, but also our resistance to death. Unless otherwise resolved, at times goodness is conceived as our desire to live forever; demons are much deeper expressions of our fears of death. Nonetheless, Burley (2008a; 2008b) redefines Silverstein's thesis, explaining that people today fear death simply because belief in heaven has declined. The secular beliefs that marked the outset of thana-capitalism neglected "the possibility of end" to the extent to adopt the needs of eternal life on earth.

As the previous argument given, the needs of embracing religion were originally questioned by *contractualism* in philosophers such as Thomas Hobbes or Jean Jacques Rousseau. Contractualism offered an innovative thesis to discuss conflict. As Hobbes observed, to avoid the war of all against all, middle-men endorse the authority to a third actor who legally monopolizes the use of force (Hobbes, 1998; Jenkins, 2008). In different levels after Hobbes, the notion of sovereignty was strictly associated with the nation-state. At the time, conflict was considered an uncivilized way of behavior, other derived archetypes surfaced. Following this explanation, for some authors, Lucifer and evilness in any state would be a scape-goat in order for members to sublimate their constrained violence (Thomas, 1978; Evans-Pritchard, 1929). In next section, we will discuss in depth the roots and nature of evilness in Abrahamic tradition with a focus on Christianity and Judaism.

## Deciphering the Mask of Evilness

For popular parlance, Lucifer shapes as a monster, many of his treats come from Pan who was a mythological creature who sexually attacked travellers in the forest or vulnerable women. However, instead of Pan in Mediterranean world, Lucifer is a major malignant figure who threatens the salvation of human souls. Instead, for some others, devil is chosen as the easiest way to reach everything what is limited in society, power, wealth and love. Celebrating a convent with Satan implies a counter-balance force that legitimizes the good-exchange circuits. In this vein, demonology and economy are inextricably intertwined. To put this in other terms, whether the circulation of goods (within economies) cements the configuration of politics, hierarchies among kinships or future ethnical conflicts, one must specu-late in this game there is losers and winners. Those values which are not affordable to those members of Western societies are wealth, love and life. In this context, devil or demons offer an alternative way for obtaining benefits otherwise would remain neglected by the lower classes. In this respect, Aragones Estella (2006) suggests that exchanging intangible commodities (as soul) by alienable goods (as wealth), demon operates in the sphere of a semi-formal circuit to strengthen the current economic order. This is the reason why it remains important to discuss Lucifer (beyond the theology) into the world of production.

Christianity and its scatology remind that evilness (Lucifer) cannot be destroyed, but few hints about why this happens. Following Ezekiel 28: 14–20 highlights the perfection of Lucifer who was originally created as protector not only of sacred temple, but also from humankind. By his attachment to trade, he was corrupted, falling into the worst sin, defiance against God.

To discuss the sin further, corruption is a key factor that symbolizes the nega-tive effects of evilness in humanity, but far from being in agreement with this con-clusion, other scholars as Slavoj Žižek understands Christianity was the first sect to pose imperfection as an acceptable cultural value. Since Christ was betrayed, there is no other reasonable paths toward salvation unless by betrayal. This cos-mology resulted in the belief that deviants should not be eradicated as in other mythologies, but exiled to construct a confrontational force between two antagonist forces. This exactly echoes with observations of Merleau-Ponty (1964), who claimed that the Catholic Church monopolized sin and forgiveness to administer salvation to its members. Every sinner who is in quest of redemption needs forgiveness to continue in its deviant attitude. In that way, institutions not only discipline parishioners but construct its hegemony by the imposition of sacred law. Philosopher Schuster noted, our current uncanny obsession with Demon stems from the needs of suppressing suffering or the pain derived from an unjust universe that transcends our individual crave. We have been educated to think if we make the correct thing we will be happy, but this does not happen in the real world. Sometimes, good people face disastrous tragedies in the same way, evildoers can be supported with a wonderful and well-deserve life. If we see disasters as a punishment of God, inevitably we need from evilness to explain the cognitive imbalance produced by our education (Schuster, 2006).

In this way, Mackendrick (2009) offers a fresh complementary argument in this discussion. The discourse of evilness has elements which can be studied in conjunction or separately to understand its multi-faceted metamorphosis. The first and most important is impurity, in the sense given by Douglas, which confers the idea of repugnance to be avoided. The monstrosity, as the second factor, works as "scapegoat" to regulate the uncertainness present in the system. The femininity as well, is pitted to patriarchal order as a sign of corruption, for example, the witch. Last but not least, the fourth element, the genocide systemizes the obliteration of otherness. British historian Margaret Deanesly (1976) reminds that witch-crafts and sorcery were unacceptable heresies punished by death in Middle Age. The traffic with Satan where witches invoked the presence of demons was possible because of their vulnerability and pervasive nature. Even, the women, for medieval theologians, were impatient creatures very influential by the devil. In her study of Deuteronomy, Douglas evinces that the meaning of impurity resonates in almost all cultures (although in different ways). As sacred fear, taboo exhibits the attempts to protect those commodities which are economically scarce for community (a type of reservoir) which turns out vital for the subsistence of society. In the rites of exorcism, Douglas adheres, each demon has the counter-effect of an archangel who voids the possession. In doing so, bodies enter in a balanced state of rest, while believers renovate their faith in the Lord.

## Understanding Witchcraft

The inception and evolution of witchcraft in Europe was based on two major events. The bulls of Innocent VIII (*Sumnis Desideratnes affectibus*) exhibited the power and liberty given to inquisition in its struggle with Satan. At second order, *Malleus Malleficarum* originally authored by two monks who devoted their life to the needs of creating a manual for identifying the servants of devil, paved the pathways for the inception of seminal demonological literature. By these days, natural disasters, misfortune, virus outbreaks or famines were signs of evil presence and of course called for the intervention of Inquisitors (Thomas, 1978). Although witches were not executed by what they did, nor by their direct actions, but only for what they thought, González-Marín (2005) adds, it is tempting to say that patriarchal European society debated its hegemony at stake when women defied the existent status quo or in case a brilliant idea threatened to change the social fabric. Revealing that evilness shares an economic nature, Comaroff and Comaroff (1993) delineate a model to understand witchcraft as a counter-response to the advance of modernity. Witchcrafts and its uses revitalize the psychological frustrations brought by colonialism in South Africa. The struggle of natives with modernity resulted in rituals of power and negotiations where magic plays a vital role. In his insight book, *Modernity and its malcontents*, they connote the economic nature evilness, colonization and witchcraft. The European colonialism not only tightens the dependency of center with its periphery by means of an economical exploitation, but it created a dichotomy between civilized vs. pagan, we vs. they, rational vs. irrational. The other non-European was subject to a conquest which encompassed a strong symbolic dependency. Austen (2010) clarifies that the notion of witches in Africa is not the same which has been employed in Europe.

> "The African Conception of the witch is tied to various forms of belief in a world where the apparent production of new wealth depends upon appropriating the scare reproductive resources of others while collaborating with an arbitrary and destructing external power. The European vision of Witchcraft is no less frightening, but it assumes an abundance rather than scarcity of the sexual energies required for reproduction."
>
> (Austen, 2010, p. 278)

Tracing the origins of European witchcraft to the discovery of Americas, Campagne (2009) sheds light on the fact that during the 15th century almost 50,000 persons were executed. These trials and executions oscillated from Germany toward France. In Germany, the half of condemned cases was women while it subtly varied in other nations. What is important to discuss, Campagne adheres, is the fact that the encounter of New and Old Worlds was not only troublesome, but very difficult event to digest. Satan served as a catalyst in order for the non-European Others to be disciplined, civilized and controlled. Those who were in contrast to the law of Medieval and Catholic rule were bloody punished to levels that may affect readers' sensibility. The archetype of witch corresponded with unaccepted practices as cannibalism, heresy or any other unauthorized cult in aboriginal tribes. Emily Oster (2004) goes on the correct side at claiming the decline of economic order and the multiplication of witch trials keep direct correlation. In a world governed by men, witches were employed as scapegoats to cover the material asymmetries and inequalities that may very well threaten the elite. In this respect, in a seminal text, entitled *The Devil in the Shape of Woman*, Carol Karlsen argues convincingly that evilness has a disciplinary goal which is selectively used or ignored to protect the interests of patriarchal society. Centered her diagnosis on valuable statistics of trials and executions, Karlsen (1987) suggests that medieval peasants avoided any contact with damned-witched not only by the fear, but also because they inspired real disasters as massive death of babies, or cattle, natural disasters or calamities of other natures. However, this seems not to be the point, she examines statistics that proofs wealthier women or those who had not offspring were targeted as the main responsible of disasters, since they celebrated a pact with the demon. Since medieval societies were based on economies of subsistence where inheritance should be kept by males, those women who lacked of children or sons would be accused of witchcraft. In perspective, the problem of witchcraft corresponds with a question of fertility and material inheritance. Furthermore, it is interesting to discuss the context where these allegations arise. In the whole of cases, trial started after a baby was found death at home, or the community faced harvest famines. Similar remarks can be replicated in the fieldwork of Rae (2008) in Nigeria, Africa. Those agents in the community accused of doing witchcraft keeps a similar profile, all they are defying the status quo, attempting to expand their hegemony, wealth and power over the rest. Whenever the circle of men is in jeopardy, the concept of "witchcraft" is used as a conceptual discourse to repress the deviants. As Karlsen puts it, the problem whether the economic asymmetries cannot be solved, the social trust runs the risk of collapse. Keith Thomas acknowledges that

> "In a society technologically more backward than ours the immediate attraction of the belief in witchcraft is not difficult to understand. It served as a mean of accounting for the otherwise inexplicable misfortunate of daily life. Unexpected disasters—the sudden death of a child, the loss of a cow, the failure of some routine household task—all could, in default of any more obvious explanation be attributed to the influence of some malevolent neighbor."
>
> (Thomas, 1978: 638)

Not surprisingly, movies such as *The Exorcist* (1973) starring Linda Blair inaugurated a widely spread fears against the demon in the United States. The tradition of New England has enrooted in the formation of a strong character where sin, conversion and service has further influence. Harry Stout in his book *The New England Soul* argues that the hearts of first ministers in New England were fulfilled by their devotion to a God which celebrated a "covenant" with the uphill city. The figure of evil was very important for these incomers in a new world not only to renovate their trust in God, but also its forgiveness. From that moment onwards, Americans as an exemplary nation chosen by God will appellate to evilness as a form of reconversion (redemption) to continue their respect for the law (Stout, 1986).

Equally important, cultural entertainment has devoted considerable attention to the figure of the devil, in most cases possession attacks young maiden or ladies who are in the twilight between childhood and adolescence. In this respect, the question of fertility plays a crucial role in the configuration of the archetype of Satan. The antichrist defined as the prince or the son of the devil will come to earth to rein for overall governments. The synopsis of these movies portrays how an ancient evil deity choses a young virgin girl to fertilize or to possess. The stage of the *Exorcist: The Beginning* (2004), where the son of the chief of the tribe is birthed dead, with thousands of worms around its body, is interesting. This sign prompted the declaration of war between the African tribe and British legion settled in the zone. To better understand this point, it is necessary to explore the origin of Lucifer's downfall.

Although discussed in the main circles of theology and philosophy, the citation of Lucifer in the Old and New Testaments is marginal. Some apocryphal texts such as the Urantia book or Enoc (the book of Watchers) gives some hints on the intersection of corruption and fertility.

Lucifer was a privileged angel, almost perfect, created to protect the sacred hill. As one of the most loved angels of heaven, he was corrupted by envy and eagerness. Gradually losing his creator's grace, Lucifer defied the power and authority of God to rule the universe. This rebellion was defeated by archangel Michael, and Lucifer was ultimately exiled, long with other fallen angels, to hell, from where they will seduce humankind. Other similar stories such as the Book of Enoch (The Watchers) or Samael's legends. It is interesting to discuss the role of fertility in the Book of Enoch. Like Lucifer, Shemihaza is created to care for humankind. However, Shemihaza and his angels desire female humans, who gave birth to giants known as Nephilims. These monsters not only devoured everything in their wake, but also wreaked havoc in earth, instilling fear throughout the four corners of the world. The watchers were punished and God dispensed a flood to purify the earth. What are the commonalities between Enoch's and Urantia's books?

Doubtless, in both cases, fertility seems to be the core element to take into consideration. At a first glance, Lucifer is the first son of God. Unlike other mythologies, where parents and sons struggle to death, in Abrahamic religions this does not pose a valid answer. God not only forgets the life of Lucifer, but also creates a dialectic by which means life is renovated. See, for example, Greek or German myths where politics and conflicts are the main value of society; rather, in Judaism and Christianity, parents are mandated to preserve the life of their offspring. From Alexander the Great to Agamemnon, the Mediterranean mythology is fraught of stories where parents assassinate their daughters and sons. This happens simply because not only does God never intervene in the problems of men, but also the king, as a commander, does what he should do. The death of sons was an unquestionable reality in Ancient Greece. She, death, was a possibility as well as a precondition to legitimate the character of an official. Of course, remorse and sin were not valid options for ancient Greeks. Instead, in Semitic cultures offspring should be protected by parents since anyone (excepting God) has the right to kill. The figure of exile played a vital role configuring the necessary punishment parents may exert over deviant sons. Not only is Abraham unable to sacrifice his beloved son, but also God's hands are tied to effacing the wayward Lucifer. It is important not to lose the sight that in Semitic cultures, the neglect of execution of offspring opens the doors for introducing the idea of "renewal" which seems to be conducive to strengthen the kinship-exchange. However, since parents are discouraged from killing their sons, a secondary state surfaces: *the neglect of death of sons*. The question of whether Lucifer is forgiven as a proof of benevolence, so that faith is renovated in a new life (redemption), is resolved in the thesis that evilness is philosophically situated as a reminder of our impossibility to die. To put this bluntly, those believers who endorse their faith in almighty God live forever. What has been discussed in earlier sections raises the question, why has God forgiven Lucifer's life?

Given this question, the answer lies within the cosmology of believers. God introduces the conception of exile-forgiveness to mediate between the creator and his creatures. Lucifer's exile from heaven produces a gap between God and Evilness which is fulfilled by faith. Christians devote their love to God knowing that evilness/sin deserves to be forgiven. The combination sin-forgiveness-sin expresses the roots of renovation where believers make their belief stronger. These cycles of eternal renovation place believers asunder from death. Starting from the idea that sons of God live forever, they neglect the possibility children may die. If the glory of God rests on the promise of eternal life, this denotes an act of renovation, which can be done only if Lucifer leads people to sin. Lucifer is forgiven not only to prove God's benevolence, but also to renew the combination of sin and forgiveness to a new life (redemption). Given the problem in these terms, the evilness becomes philosophically our reminder about the impossibility to die. In sharp contrast with Žižek, who argues that Christianity rests on the needs of betrayal, we hold the thesis that Christianity-Capitalism evolved by the "neglect the death of sons." Quite aside from the polemic, which deserves further research, we have connoted the intersection of economy and evilness, highlighting the possibility that Lucifer-witchcraft was the channel to balance problems of fertility in society.

## Conclusion

Preliminary, this essay-review situated the specialized literature under the lens of critical scrutiny. In opposition to what has been written, we hold the thesis that Lucifer or evilness represents a repressed idea imposed by capitalist culture, where the death of sons is rejected. The studies of historians or enthnographers who have focused on witchcraft agree that evilness serves as a scapegoat to protect the productive system of some derived glitches, which should be corrected. Since wealthier women represented a serious problem for patriarchal medieval society, not surprisingly the execution of witches was a disciplinary mechanism of control. Additionally, interesting assumptions can be made when comparing Greek and Christian mythologies. Lucifer, who was the first son of God, was exiled to produce a "dialectic" between God and Evil, which served the purposes of believers. God forgives Lucifer to renew the faith between his grace and the chosen peoples. The question whether Christendom offered the possibility to reach eternal life (unlike Greeks or Ancient Germans) associates with the presence of demons.

The binomial sin-forgiveness-sin denotes renovation, which instills the hope that the son of God lives forever. If we as sons of the Lord will live forever, we understand our sons cannot die. Whenever the sense of reality is imposed on our dreams, fear emerges. From the fears in this world there is no word to express what a parent feels whenever his or her offspring dies. Even in language there is no term to denote the status of a person who has lost children. This reflection invites readers to consider the roots of evilness from an innovative and fresh angle, which hopefully continues in the next approaches. At the time Christianity paved the way for the advance and consolidation of thana-capitalism, the death of sons was a harsh reality previously unconceived.

# 6    From the Enigma of Christ Toward Noah's Ark

## Introduction

Over the centuries, theologians have adamantly debated on the mystery of Christ to grasp the dichotomy between evilness and goodness. At a closer look, the message says that God sent his most loved son to be sacrificed by humanity, as a proof of his immense love and benevolence. At some point, from Adam and Eve on, humankind was bereft by the Fall in a way that threatened its salvation. The problem with this conception of divinity was that God needs to transform his omnipotence into a vulnerable creation in order to repeat the original message which was not correctly understood by humankind. In this vein, Noah's ark and the myth of Christ's crucifixion are inextricably intertwined.

As in the previous argument given in Chapter 3, Slavoj Žižek, who is a Slovenian philosopher well recognized for his contributions to modern philosophy, introduces a radical reading of capitalism and mass consumption with a focus on the role of Christianity as a configuration of the modern law. His original position combines the most polemic aspects of Lacanian psychoanalysis with post-Marxian studies. In this vein, Žižek exerts an interesting criticism against the economy of desires, which is enrooted in the allegories of consumption. When I came across the book *The Puppet and the Dwarf* and its discussion of the perverse core of Christianity, I thought that Žižek placed the process of anthropomorphization under the lens of scrutiny (along the same lines as Weber or Sombart), but I was wrong. His development is much deeper than this and of course invites a hot debate. The tergiversation of the message starts with Paul, not with Christ. The question is, why?

In perspective, Žižek suggests that not only does Paul's doctrine pave the way for the institutionalization of the Catholic Church, but also it intersected the message with the politics of nation-sate. If theorists of secularization think that religion is in decline, there is no doubt for Žižek that they are completely mistaken. The world of beliefs is more valid and active than ever. If nation-states evince less influence from the Catholic Church than in earlier times, this does not mean that human beliefs are next to disappear. This happens, Žižek observes, because religions play an ambiguous role in the configuration of society as well as its ways of producing politics. On one hand, it helps laypeople living in a constructive and more sustainable way, but on another it poses a restrictive cosmology in practitioners to understand the world. From the Medieval Age to the Enlightenment, even if religions had different meanings according to others times and cultures, no less true is that in this contemporary society, religion is reserved for private life alone. In this respect, Christianity kept a perverse core which only can be deciphered by means of materialism. Unless otherwise resolved, modernism not only accepts religiosity only to produce a cultural entertainment also fictionalizes its main content in stereotyped forms of consumption such as films, the arts or architecture. At a closer look, through the reading of any text, the quotation marks serve to show readers that the paragraphs or the ideas within them express others' opinion. This shows not only we preserve our faith, but also the sense of credibility is given by what is written alone. The use of quotation marks helps distinguish what is credible from what is not. As this backdrop, Žižek adheres to the thesis we have a blind faith in everything that can be visually tested. This raises a more than interesting question: Why Žižek and why now?

First and foremost, understanding the archetype of Christ represents a fertile ground to gain further explanations on how thana-capitalism has established and evolved but secondly, far from being an act of love, the crucifixion of Christ exhibits the first attempt for Occident to theatralize other's suffering, a common-thread argument in this book.

Returning to Žižek, let's explain that there is a gap between the real Christ in history and his mythical figure, which is fulfilled by cultural consumptions. Nowadays, the industries of cultural entertainment and tourism endorse a sacred veil to religion and its icons only if they can be commoditized by cultural consumption. Starting from the premise of what is gazed at obtains worth, Žižek says that a global audience is shocked whenever ancient icons of Buddhism are destroyed by jihadists not because we share our solidarity with this religion, but because these are masterpieces or objects of art which merit protection. Everything which is associated with cultural consumption is prioritized over others' values. What is more than important to discuss is why those aspects of cultures which cannot be commoditized are not covered by the media.

## The Perverse Core of Christianity

As stated, the perverse core of Christianity consists in subordinating all mainstream values to politics, which seems to be articulated with the end of preventing local revolutions. In this stage, the act of betrayal fulfils a decisive role in determining the passage from mortality to eternal life. If Christ becomes in God, this happens because he is betrayed by Judas, which means that Christianity was expanded as the main ideology of the West only to encourage "betrayal" as a significant aspect of contemporary society. Since cults and religions promote the loyalty of peoples to goodness, Christianity goes in the inverse direction. Before their being resurrected, God asks humans to be betrayed, tortured and crucified in a way that leads him to redeem all sins. In recent decades, scholars with expertise in comparative religions understood that humans construct their gods not only to conform to their image, but also to project their psychological frustrations upon. The twilight of the gods starts whenever humans ignore or defy their authorities. If secularism reminds us of something, it consists in denouncing the arbitrariness of gods, which led humankind to adopt a much deeper rational thinking. However, in the mythology of Christianity, God (who is embodied as Christ) asks humankind to be abandoned, replaced by the suffering of witnessing the son's death. Žižek is not wrong when says that Christ emulates the inversion of Job's suffering, at the time God and the devil agree to inflict pain on Job only for their pleasure. Job replied to God, If you do not make nothing to alleviate my suffering, you will have nothing to do when your son faces the same calvary. The same can be found in other myths of Christianity such as the creation of Adam and Eve. The founding parents are banned to eat from only one tree while almost all of creation remains at their disposal. This suggests that from its inception creation is linked to the Fall. As discussed in Chapter 5, God created Lucifer in the same way as Adam and Eve not only to validate his supremacy, but also to forgive them to produce a philosophical dialectic between the sin and forgiveness. In that way, Christianity not only paves the way for the rise of discipline, but also neglects the probabilities of dying. In this vein Merleau-Ponty (1964) discussed to what extent the Catholic Church legitimized its authority by the imposition of sin, which sublimated the soul by means of forgiveness (a moot point Žižek echoes). This means that politics and dialectics are inextricably intertwined. For example, militant pro-abortionists and atheists who denounced the arbitrariness of Catholic Church fall themselves in the same acts once power is originally embraced. While fundamentalist terrorists attack the secular culture, they become themselves agents of the capitalism they struggle to defeat (Žižek, 2003). This is a proof of the existence of Hegelian dialectics at the core of capitalist society. The problem of dialectics was historically examined by many philosophers and social scientists; however, fewer studies focused on its intersection with fear. In his book *The Dialectics of Social Thought*, Geoffrey Skoll (2014) brilliantly presents a fresh and innovative thesis about the dialectics of agency and society. No matter the status of two agents, or the value each one gains in the market, the fact is that both are determined by the social dialectics that precede them. Outside of society, the agent has no significance, while society loses its reason to exist without human agency. What Skoll discusses is the functionality of both elements to delineate their respective importance for the system. Rich people need from the low-status workers as the latter ones need from the capital-owner. To overcome the conflicts of those dialectics, engender, Skoll suggests that the social order is based, following Simmel, on a triadic structure. The process of negotiation between two or more pillars alludes to the existence of a third, where the dialectical relationship is based on negations. From its inception, philosophy and social sciences are orchestrated to produce a dialectic between two sides, which was conducive to the bourgeois and the capitalist system. To validate this, Skoll proposes that social "thought" as a text sheds light on the world by employing Hegel's dialectic, simply because the concept of the social is dialectic by its nature. Two of the senior scholars who have realized on this were Freud and Marx, who devoted considerable time and effort in elucidating the invisible ties that keep society united. From diverse views, both acknowledged the "reification of reason" as the primary goal of social scaffolding. Though they lived in different times, Freud emphasized neurotic self-deception; Marx focused on the mystification of political economy. As in society, the constitution of the self corresponds with a reification between rules and drives. Most certainly, it is safe to say that Ego is for Freud, what Capital is for Marx. What is the ghost in the machine of capitalism? With a closer look, capital mediates between production and workers just as ego corresponds with the interplay between repression and reason. The main thesis of this brilliant work is that social diagnosis about the problems of reproduction is based on dialectics since it is social. When just two individuals interact this dynamic is impossible to study. This raises other questions: How can society be a unified object? Are human beings social in nature?

Sociology, over the years, attempted to respond to these questions by alluding to the figure of the city as the recipient of human relations. Any metropolis condenses the accumulation of human resources, capital and production, and it expresses the dialectics of machines and the workforce. What Skoll dissects is that the social bondage is based on the dialectic from its inception. With a great erudition, the radical development through this book reveals two interesting concerns. First and foremost, the dialectics of triadic thought was applied to "social understanding" in all social thinkers from pragmatists to nihilists. Secondly, the modern social order based on the dialectic generated the monopoly of meaning of capitalism juxtaposing two modes of thinking. At the bottom, social sciences delineated the original adoption of the capitalist view which exploits agency toward an irreversible stage of collapse.

From a deep critique of Marx, as formulated by Skoll in the preliminary sections, the book passes in the third chapter to the epistemological problems in Hegel and Freud. One of the aspects that characterized psychoanalysis was the belief that behavior is the expression from unknown spheres of humanity, from unconsciousness. Far from being the subject, subjectivity becomes an "object" to be placed under the lens of expert scrutiny. The "laypeople" are educated to understand themSelves, through the mediation of the analyst. This type of analytic process consists of getting away the mythical autonomy of agency to achieve a view of other much deeper forces. The reading of the fourth chapter suggests that pragmatism adopted the same argument by confirming that the world is a simulacrum which rests on the interaction of actors. The theory of dialectics, though extended in academic circles, is conducive to the status quo sliding in meeting its responsibilities. The interwar period paved the way for the advent of the Frankfurt school which generated a real revolution in the West. In perspective, this school employed the dialectics of history to expand its understanding of revolts and social breaks. Once again, the social scientists influenced by post-Marxian legacy questioned the capitalist system by adopting its primary epistemology. Last but not least, Skoll recognizes that phenomenology cannot persist without the use of dialectics as it has been discussed in this review. Precisely, this led analysts to ignore three main social problems: ecology, terrorism and economy. If terrorism can be understood as a "commoditization of fear," the exhaustion of local resources by capitalism creates the conditions for the current condition of crisis. Terrorism diverts attention from real problems produced by capitalism and its inevitable collapse. As a concept which can be manipulated, fear may be commoditized not only to break the law, but also to exert a disciplinary mechanism in which the citizenry accepts policies that they otherwise would reject. These abstractions can be drawn according to the interests of the status quo.

> "Security and terrorism are bound together in a dialectical process of mutually defining each other; they create each other in economic and environmental turmoil. What the process produces is the national state of securitization, continual terrorist incidents, and an ever growing market for security goods and services. Despite its apparent self-generating dynamic, the terrorism dynamic is part of a larger whole with links to the economic process and the biophysical environment. Terrorism, like anti-Communism and crime fighting are political faces of larger social processes." (Žižek, 2003, p. 116)

This cyclical process, as Žižek puts it, cannot be understood behind Christianity, since it prohibits the expression of enjoyment. Christianity gives to humans the hopes of a better life, but the precondition is based on the needs of contriving the inner crave. Unlike other religions, Christianity promised us that the true happiness rests on our impossibility to fulfil the desire contriving self-consciousness. Since individuals are unfamiliar with the expression of their desires, they do not understand the effects of their individual decision-making process. To wit, Žižek's account, though with many limitations, is interesting in that it paved the way to the theory of thana-capitalism, a new stage of modern production, where death becomes the main commodity. Thana-capitalism situates a new climate characterized by the presence of social institutions that regulate interaction by exposing others' death. From journalism to TV programs, films and realities, the West has commoditized death as a new form of entertainment for the global audience to remain under control. Doubtless, Christianity and suffering are historically interlinked. This ethical dilemma was widely exploited by jihadists who have captivated the strange fascination of the modern audience for disaster-related news. While consuming terrorism through media, Westerners developed an aversion to terrorism, but they cannot stop consuming terrorism-led news.

## Thana-Capitalism and the Image of Death

In earlier works such as *A Difficult World* (Korstanje, 2015) I argued polemically that capitalism was successfully expanded thanks to two main ideas. The first is the belief that people want to feel different, special, outstanding, the unique in a race in which only one winner takes everything. Secondly, social Darwinism, which poses as the platform where competitors understand and which others are worthy of being the winners. In fact, thana-capitalism, a term derived from thanatos, which means death, widely broadcasts the death of others in order for the audience to feel secure and happy: after all, they are still alive, although in a race that sooner or later will have no winner. Of course, participants in these

Darwinist scenarios are not only unfamiliar with their real probabilities to win, but also embrace narcissism as the narcotic that helps them overcome their daily frustrations. The individual's happiness is any longer determined by his or her own achievements, as it was in the times of wayward puritans, but by the pain of others—in which case a new logic surfaces.

Michaud, analogically, introduces the term "luxury of experiences" to discuss the climate of narcissism where people want to feel superior to others who had not the same luck. Michaud starts from the premise that "traditional luxury" that is known as a disposition to acquire curious objects of collection sets the pace to a new type, more oriented to "experiences." In this luxury, associated to individual sensations, subjects are in quest of outstanding and unique experiences such as those of an African safari, a trip to the moon or a stay in one of the expensive hotels of the world. Citing Veblen, Michaud clarifies that this type of conspicuous consumption is based on two significant factors. The need of boasting, to feel special or superior to others, is conjoined with the quest for "authentic experiences." Anthropologically speaking, as Michaud adheres, luxury as an institution traversed across cultures and times, producing a political hierarchy between officialdom and the members of the tribe. Paradoxically, consumers seek to experience outstanding sensations to make a substantial difference from others who are financially limited only to survival. Citizens of the first world travel to "paradisiacal destinations" to get outstanding experiences, whereas the local low-income workforce is exploited by eager global investors who see these destinations as good opportunities to maximize their profits. Investment in tourist destination erodes the security in the labor of locals paying lower wages than in Europe or the United States. The segmentation of consumers and marketing in particular are interested in stimulating outstanding experiences. In doing so, the landscapes of destinations are externally designed not only to be ideologically disposed toward holiday-makers, but also representing a renewable resource which never ends. To put this in other terms, its volatile attributes feeds the untrammelled consuming machine to engender an "addictive character." The original and its copycat are two sides of the same coin. While the former after remaining in secrecy should be unveiled by discoverers, an act that excites travellers, the latter signals the humdrum routine of daily life. Whatever the case may be, in the final section, Michaud argues that luxury and tourism are inextricably intertwined, but both follow divergent goals. Last but not least, tourists are always pressed by their need to experience pleasurable events, consuming local culture and identities in order to find themselves. In retrospect, luxury endorses pleasure to consumers within a circle of exceptionality by reinforcing a fragile character that needs to experience authenticity to feel superior to others (Michaud, 2015).

## The Enigma of Christ

One of the aspects that define Žižek's development is associated to his materialism, or atheism, when handling issues related to theologians. His position was fruitful since it explains further on how egoism leads human will to struggle with others to survive, a very well point we have already developed through this text. Basically, Žižek understands that Christianity not only ideologically legitimizes "the betrayal" but also situates the concept of danger in a world which has been created to be venerated. However, much attention should be given to the archetype of Christ in comparison to a secondary myth Žižek left behind, Noah's Ark. In consequence, Žižek is certainly obsessed to show the problem comes from Christianity, when really it is much older. Since Noah stems from the Old Testament, accepting his intersection with Christ would show the inconsistencies of Žižek's own theory.

Not surprisingly, cinema and cultural entertainment have portrayed Noah as almost a hero, a new founder who endorsed the grace of God as a protector of life. The world of Cain, which degenerated into a climate of corruption, despair and sin, was expiated by the divine rage, while Noah is asked to fabricate an ark to save the life on earth. After all, he is invested as the only survivor who witnesses the total obliteration, the spectacle of disaster dispensed by God. The reason why Noah gained much glory and acceptance in the West is associated with the fact that it reminds us of two major assumptions. The first is that no matter what humans, God always will protect the founding kinship in order for our species to be preserved. In fact, this exciting allegory feeds a sentiment of supremacy where humankind is presented as the center, the administrator of the universe. If they did or made the wrong decision, everything can be solved, protecting the life of only one. Doubtless, this myth works as the symbolic platform for the rise of thana-capitalism and the spectacles of suffering thousands of tourists are prone to gaze on and consume. What Noah reminds us is that only one can win, while the rest of unworthy humanity should be doomed. A second point of entry in this discussion is the case of Christ, who, unlike Noah, is the son of God.

Christ attempts to dissuade humans that the only way to salvation is not suffering or purification, but love. The cruelty of the god of the Old Testament sets the pace to a new benevolent deity, who not only becomes human, but also lives in conditions of poverty and humility. At the time Christ was crucified, the world understood two things. One on hand, the rich are not worthy to enter heaven unless they discard all their wealth, which means they consume all their objects on earth (mass consumerism). Secondly, the shocking figure of Christ as a tortured person not only expresses an extreme suffering, reminding that all so-called messiahs and prophets should be subject to an unspeakable tribulation, but cements the possibility to orchestrate a show of suffering, which was revitalized by than-capitalism. Christianity is the only religion whose sacred figure is a dying subject barbarically hanging on a crux. In one of the conferences of religion I attended, one Buddhist colleague shared with me his disturbance on seeing how Christ was crucified; he told me, "Do you know how disgusting and shocking is witnessing how a person is nailed to a crux to die slowly?" This not only seems to be a sign of Westerner sadism, but a precondition to eternal love. Whatever the case may be, Christ ignites the discussion around the problem of suffering as a sign of exception. Last but not least, Christ divides the world in two, what falls as victims of arbitrariness, and those who, moved by curiosity, need only to gaze at the suffering of others. One world rests on the needs of sacrifice, which means the restriction of pleasure to achieve a collective world. Rather, the second signals to the maximization of hedonism escaping through others' pain from the one condition which is irreversible, death. This tendency that has been accelerated in late capitalism paved the way for the advance of thana-capitalism, a tendency where the suffering of others is the main commodity, or cultural value, to consume. Unlike what Žižek precludes, we feel that Christianity constrained the problem of hedonism, until the rise of anti-modernist through the ninetheen century, a radical shift of cosmologies which granted the passage from the producerist society to a new society where consumption and hedonism prevailed. As Jackson Lears observed, the problem of pain and self-constraint was always present in puritanism, a cosmology which facilitated the expansion of capitalism worldwide. Although Max Weber was a pioneer in finding that the cosmology of puritans was the touchstone of capitalism, what remaine less clear is to what extent a sect that struggled for an inner life, hard work and self-constraint came, over the course of a few decades, to transform into a hegemonic empire based on mass consumption and social Darwinism. The answer leads us toward the claim of antimodernists for the problems and pathologies that the liberal market produces in daily life. Taking his cue from cultural studies, Lears (1994) examines the roots of modern capitalism as the need for the human body to recoil from pain. If the mind covers irrational drives, which should be punished for puritan view, antimodernists went in the opposite direction: they believed not only in the autonomy of self, but also in the expression of individual emotions. Antimodernists fulfilled the role of intermediary agents between harsh puritanism and frugal capitalism. Instead of being oppressed by the world of beliefs, humans should launch a quest to discover new experiences, to the authenticity of their sensations. In that way, they not only revitalized the world of personal achievement but also endorsed the importance of consumption. The growing climate of rationality and oppression sooner resulted in new cases of neurasthenia which were therapeutically treated by means of psychiatry and psychology. This endemic disease surfaced throughout the nineteenth century, pressed for a cultural crisis of authority which has no precedents in the world of the capitalist system. This crisis not only opened the doors of the puritan soul for the advance of consuming life, but the desire to make on earth a real paradise. In so doing, governments should devote resources to support the scientific research, which paradoxically threatened the main belief of the Old and New Testaments, first and foremost around the idea of creationism that was pitted against social Darwinism. Lears goes on to say,

"Antimodernists did more than revitalize older bourgeois values of activism and achievement; they also helped to transform those values. This transformation stemmed less from class determinants than from the nature of the dissent itself. In a secularizing culture, where larger frameworks of meaning were fading, the anti-modern quest for real life often focused on the self alone; intense experience became an end in itself. Sentimentalizing emotional spontaneity and instinctual vitality, much anti-modernism displayed the limits common to fin-de-siecle vitalism; it also melded with new style therapies of abundance and some versions of corporate liberal social engineering." (Lears 1994, p 58)

The same applies for what Richard Hofstadter stated in his classic book, *Social Darwinism in American Thought,* regarding to the rise of a new race (Anglo-Saxons), who not only defied the conceptual tenets of religion which are replaced by progress and struggle, but also speaks on behalf of an ethnocentric idea where some are entitled to survive while others simply perish. In his development, he acknowledges that one of the primary aspects that was determined by competition and the spirit of entrepreneurs in the United States was the adoption of social Darwinism per the view of authors such as Asa Gray, Graham Sumner and Herbert Spencer. This biological theory postulated two significant axioms which reinforced the sentiment of excemptionalism inherited in the founding parents of nation. The first was the "survival of fittest"; the second was "social determinism." In a brilliant argument, Hofstadter proposes that the legitimacy of law to ensure the equality of all citizens was not sufficient to explain why some actors are successful while others falls in ruins. As a supra-organism, the social structure overrides the interpretation of law. To evolve to a better stage, the society should accept the struggle for survival as the primary cultural value. The social advance depends on the wealth heritage one generation can pass to another. In this view, "primitive man, who long ago withdrew from the competitive struggle and ceased to accumulate capital goods, must pay with a backward and unenlightened way of life" (p. 58).

Millionaires do not result from greed or avarice, but from the evolution of natural selection. They have been selected by their strengths, tested in their success in business, and abilities to achieve adaptation to environment. Rather, others have been relegated to occupy poor conditions of existence or to disappear. Because social Darwinism was a doctrine originally adopted by some religious waves, not only Sumner but also Gray warned of the negative effects of leaving the poor without assistance. However, both agree that states cannot promote charity as a governmental policy; if this happens it runs the risks of decline. The society should be recycled, allowing the big fish to eat the small fish. The question that Hofstadter assertively formulates is, why does a religion adopt these types of beliefs?

To look cloeser, Calvinist and other Protestant circles emphasized the hostility of the environment as a proof of faith. This belief suggests that man evolves in a conflictive and dangerous world. Secondly, the archetype of an uphill city which holds the selected people exerted considerable influence to delineate the roots of labor. Being successful, for Americans, was more than important to ensure one is part of those selected by God. At the surface, this is not very different from what social Darwinism historically claimed.

Likely, the lack of autonomy in Christianity was given (following Žižek) by the concept of omnipotence in which we have situated God. As a counterfactual reaction, we allude to God when things turn wrong or escape our rationality. We are in quest for explanations of events which are decided without our intervention. This is exactly what God means, Žižek adheres. The omnipotent agent often escapes, to the chagrin of puritans who believe in predestination, and cannot be reached by humans. The need to symbolize a third party as more powerful than I seems associated with the fact I depend on these remote Others' protection. Žižek writes that, "every legal power, no matter how democratic it appears, no matter how much it is constrained by laws and regulations has to be sustained by an underground echo of But ultimately, they can do whatever they want with us! Without this echo, power simply loses its authority. Does the same not hold for the divine predestination? God's decision to save some of us and to condemn others for eternity is not founded on truth and right reason … it was made simply for such was His good pleasure. Such experience of omnipotence is rooted in the small child's dependency on his/her mother, the first love object which has the inexplicable power of arbitrarily providing or withdrawing pleasure and objects which satisfy the child's needs." (Žižek, 2016: 21)—in which case it fits to our argument.

In a world of contrasts, liberality, modernity and mobilities are promoted as mainstream value of civilization, while others' cultures that do not share this are stereotyped as backward or underdeveloped. Žižek says that there is no such thing as liberty for all human beings born in egalitarian conditions, since American democracy would have never been constructed without racism against blacks. The same happens in France with respect to Islamic migrants. This forced workforce— although enthusiastic in the belief they will enter in the land of opportunities—not only are rejected but also are incorporated into a subordinated position.

In thana-capitalism, the curiosity for others' death is not very different to witnesses to Christ's tragedy. They are just there where the suffering flourishes but not to express their solidarity with the others, nor to coordinate an act of rebellion, but only to be the subject of their own narcissism. As Michaud puts it, our efforts to mark a wall dividing us from others is triggered by the need to cause envy. Luxury would work in a similar way to death. To what extent the emergent demands for visiting death spaces surfaced in England and English-speaking countries corresponds with interesting hypotheses this chapter has cleared. The "Anglo-World," which inherited the influence of Puritans, is prone to consume death as a fertile ground to legitimate the climate of Darwinism developed inside. In Catholic nations dark tourism never flourished because poverty still plays a crucial role to open heaven's doors.

## The Bottom Days and the Struggle for Survival

The zombie virus has gone viral. The cable television series *The Walking Dead* had seven million "likes" on Facebook and 300,000 Twitter followers as of March 2012 (Lazar, 2012). Vampires, if anything, show even larger numbers with an estimated 32 million Facebook "likes" (Graphs.net 2013). Other undead populate the web and popular culture. The undead in various forms may not inhabit the earth, but they proliferate and reproduce in electronic form along with print media. I suggest that this phenomenon, the popularity of undead motifs, does not arise from especially clever marketing strategies, although they play a role; they would find less success if these motifs did not resonate with a form of public consciousness, or more accurately, unconsciousness. The undead represent a post-modern sensibility. This sensibility reeks of decay.

> "[It is a] 'degraded' landscape of schlock and kitsch, of TV series and *Readers'* *Digest* culture, of advertising and motels, of the late show and the Grade-B Hollywood film, of so-called paraliterature with its airport paperback categories of the gothic and the romance, the popular biography, the murder mystery and sciencefiction or fantasy novel: materials they no longer simply 'quote,' as a Joyce or a Mahler might have done, but incorporate into their very substance." (Jameson, 1991, p. 55)

Jameson goes on to assert that postmodern culture represents a political unconscious. That is, people experience a postmodern political economy, but they lack the wherewithal to express it in articulate discourse, in political terms. In a similar vein, the arts have represented, in what might be considered prescient ways, what has already begun in the economic, political and social structures but has not yet appeared in explicit terms. Somewhat arbitrarily stated, modernism began in the mid-nineteenth century. Charles Baudelaire called it *modernité*. Accordingly, modernism depicted the ephemeral, fleeting, ever-changing nature of industrialized urbanism. Even then Baudelaire's fascination with the macabre and his admiration for the work of Edgar Allan Poe portended a certain connection between death, decay and the advent of modern culture. It is with such artistic background that another viewpoint seems relevant to the social character of the time.

Undoubtedly, the struggle for survival is not new and has been explored in classic myths such as Sophocles' *Oedipus Rex*, or in movies such as *The Walking Dead*, which presents the apocalyptic horizon of a zombie virus that expands to all the earth. Artistic work presents the most obvious, but by no means the only or even the most important, instance of human creativity. It is most obvious, because artist's work creates works—paintings, plays, symphonies, sculpture, and so on. The works objectify human creativity in ways that help us experience them as distinctive products, unlike, for example, social institutions, which are continuous and necessarily collective. Although sharing certain basic characteristics such as art, we sense glaring differences between, say, Sophocles' *Oedipus Rex* and *The Walking Dead*. Both are dramatic performances, and both present problems of their respective ages. Nonetheless, differences in media technology count for a lot in the sense that they seem quite distinct from one another. In part that difference lies with the different machinery used to produce them. A critical feature of the dramatic machinery of ancient Athens was architecture. Situated outdoors, the stage and chorus area formed the focus of stadium seating accommodating as many as 12,000 to 14,000 spectators. Since dialogue was essential, the architecture had to provide acoustics so that the thousands of spectators could hear it. This kind of architectural machinery has two important features: it is stationary and relatively permanent. Neither feature applies to *The Walking Dead*. The latter is a digitized performance enacted remotely and based on a comic book series of the same name. Audiences can see and hear it at any time or place using a variety of devices ranging from theatre-sized screens to handheld mobile telephones. The enabling machinery, satellites, remains invisible, certainly compared to the stone stadia of ancient Greece. In ancient Greece the audience participated in the performance, and the whole performance was a ritual of intensification, since the plays enacted the mythologies that served as icons of culture. The audience entered into the work of art. In television performances, and a fortiori for online videos, the audience is removed. Pace Benjamin, who said, "Architecture has always represented the prototype of a work of art the reception of which is consummated by a collectively in a state of distraction. The laws of its reception are most instructive" (Benjamin, 2005, sec.IX). In this he paralleled the Brechtian epic or, as Brecht later called it, dialectical theatre. Distraction, or escapism, was what Brecht tried to overcome by making his productions analogous to those of the ancient Greeks. One of the goals of epic theatre is for the audience to always be aware that it is watching a play: "It is most important that one of the main features of the ordinary theatre should be excluded from [epic theatre]: the engendering of illusion" (Brecht, 1964, p. 122).

In his essay "The Work of Art in the Age of Mechanical Reproduction," Walter Benjamin (1996) analyzed machine replication. His analysis aimed at a common problematic for the Frankfurt school—namely, how to explain how the German proletariat, widely considered among the most progressive if not revolutionary in the industrialized world, succumbed to the appeal of the Nazis. He and his colleagues lay the blame on mass culture and its manipulation for political ends.

> "The logical result of Fascism is the introduction of aesthetics into political life. The violation of the masses, whom Fascism, with its Führer cult, forces to their knees, has its counterpart in the violation of an apparatus which is pressed into the production of ritual values.... All efforts to render politics aesthetic culminate in one thing: war." (Benjamin, 1936, epilogue)

At least with respect to theatre, and doubtless other forms of art as well, manipulation of audiences for political purposes does not necessarily equate with fascism. Moreover, the unfortunate political consequences of the art forms have less to do with the art than their use and milieu. The political problematic does not arise from the medium, but the uses for which it is intended and the uses to which it is put, often very different things. Here one distinguishes between the mechanical reproductions of Picasso's *Guernica* as opposed to Leni Riefenstahl's *Triumph of the Will*. As to Picasso's intent, Paul Virilio reports, "When a German interrogated him in 1937 about his masterwork: 'That is your doing, not mine!'" (Virilio, 2003, p. 19). Leni Riefenstahl blamed it all on the audience.

> "I met Leni Riefenstahl and asked her about her epic films that glorified the Nazis. Using revolutionary camera and lighting techniques, she produced a documentary form that mesmerized Germans; her *Triumph of the Will* cast Hitler's spell....

"She told me that the 'messages' of her films were dependent not on 'orders from above,' but on the 'submissive void' of the German public. Did that include the liberal, educated bourgeoisie? 'Everyone,' she said." (Pilger, 2013)

Benjamin, and far less ambiguously Theodor Adorno (1997), decried the subsumption of classical artistic canons to the political economy of capitalism. Capitalism affects art the same way it affects all other aspects of social life: it alienates artists from the means of production and their works as it commodifies art, just as it does with all forms of human endeavour. In fact, art is a realm of social life less commodified than others. If there is a difference wrought between *The Walking Dead* and *Oedipus Rex*, it does not lie in their technical media, contrary to the dictum of Marshall McLuhan that "the medium is the message." The relations among artists, audience, technology, and the social, economic and political order are dialectical. They condition and in fact co-create one another. *The Walking Dead* reflects the end of the political economic order of world capitalism in much the same way as *Oedipus Rex* represented the beginning of the end of Athenian democracy. To cut a long story short, societies are constructed on basis of two contrasting forces, order and chaos. Staring from the premise the world has been created by the forces of order also the end should be in charge of chaos. The presence of death in the biological life of human beings is experienced as problematic and fearful. However, individual human beings gain immortality through their identification with and participation in their societies (Durkheim, 1984). Hence arose the belief in recycled individuals: when one dies in this world one expects to live at another level. Theories of apocalypses are often a projection of the social contexts a people is experiencing. Millenarianism is composed of two elements: the bottom-days are accompanied by a terrible fright which wreaks havoc in the populace, but with a renovation of faith and hope for the future. Early capitalism erased the utopic element of in favor of a paradise on earth where everyone could have the opportunity to live a life of abundance. Capitalism's late modern decline has ushered in a hopeless consternation, represented by a world of undead. Moral philosophy is not wrong to say that in Western history the religious belief surrounding the future has consisted in an eschatological conviction the world will abruptly end with the return of a messiah who will vindicate the poor and oppressed in his name, fighting stubbornly against their enemies. Precisely, one of the aspects fear generates in people is a lack of perspective, and uncertainty as to precisely how and when the planet will finally succumb. The metaphor of biopolitics as producer of life and death was epitomized by Nazis during WWII, but once ended, its spirit passed to the core of Americanness as it will be discussed in the next chapter.

# 7    The Supremacy of the Anglo-Race

## Individualism above All

### Introduction

One of the main obstacles to explore "thana-capitalism," consists in dealing with bio-capitalism. Even, the concept of bio-power was originally coined by social theorist Michel Foucault (2009), who was obsessed to present a conceptual model to understand the techniques used by the nation-state to administer to population, territory and life. In contrast to other political organizations, Foucault adds, modern nation-states are based on the prerogative to create life by letting others die. This technology controls threats dispersing over the bodies by the introduction of an economy of discipline. Alluding to the metaphor of viruses, Foucault argues convincingly that the power of discipline is not oriented to eradicate dangers, but to mitigate their effects in society. Whether a vaccine exhibits an inoculated virus, it shows how discipline works. Although widely cited and critically discussed, the theory of bio-capitalism was recently brought to discussion by Tim Ingold in his book *Being Alive* (2011). In this project, he gathers interesting information collated from his earlier ethnographies to present a new theory of human agency and its environment. Although the Occident devoted considerable attention to the question of life, it was based on a Cartesian dualism where the introduction of technology was tilted at dividing humans from the rest of creation. In fact, unlike hunters and gatherers, who perceive the world as a continuum, Westerners monopolized technology to reinforce their territorial attachment within sedentary forms of production. Isolated from the environment, modern science (even biology) constructed around "the self" the idea that humans should be enthralled over what nonhuman is. In that way, life and the environment were preserved only in laboratories or reservoirs duly protected from daily contact, starting from the premise that the West acknowledges human life should be disengaged from nature. As something superior, humans not only are invested to administer the earth at their discretion, but also produce a dislocation between observed object and observers. This dichotomy gave to modern science the necessary objectivity which hunters or gatherers lacks, but at the same time adopted the values of capitalism as an ever-existing reality. If today the failures of ecological policies and programs are evident, this happens because humankind has developed a "dwelling perspective" of animals. With this in mind, hunters and gatherers had a "relational perspective" of the world in which they dwell, but Westerners need mapping to be visually inserted into a specific territory. The relational views connect with nature from a closer stance, considering that humankind is enrooted in the natural life and cycles of earth. This begs a more than pungent question: Where does the concept of dwelling perspective come from?

From Martin Heidegger, Ingold takes the cue "dwelling perspective" to mean that any space is symbolically created to be dwelled in by human intervention. As this argument given, the ecology is thought as something disembodied from human agency. Moved by reason, Westerners support the Cartesian dualism to pose culture as a shelter from the external hostile world. The first ethnologists and anthropologists constructed the "sense of the other," not only in sharp opposition to Europe, but also validating the ideology of evolution which was formulated by Charles Darwin. Following adaptation of Darwinism to social Darwinism in the hands of Francis Galton, white man envisaged the world as virgin soil which merited to be conquered. The Other was a dangerous element to be disciplined according to a much deeper cultural matrix, centered on reason and instrumentality. For the European logic, the role of labor as a configurator (cosmo-creator) of social order alluded to trade as the only factor that characterized the progress of a certain civilization. In that way, capitalism not only introduces in modern Europe some substantial changes, but also recently installed a cultural project in which desire was separated from reason. This new world which comes from the rise of industrialism made the belief that things always were as today. However, far from being true, Ingold adds, capitalism is almost 300 years old. The division of labor and leisure as well as the introduction of escapement mechanisms not only were inherited to Europeanness, but also forged a specific consciousness which is associated with capitalist ethos. As he puts it, the ideological power of capitalism rested on its efficacy to mark others as exchangeable commodities. While the commodities are framed by the price which can be exchanged, the workforce is financially linked to the capacity to consume what others yield. To put things in a straight, workers are motivated to produce commodities and objects they will consume to transfer their wealth (surplus value) toward capital-owners' hands. In recent times, problems of global warming as a threatening force that places humankind in jeopardy not only cannot be reversed, but also exhibit one of the ideological contradictions of how life is culturally defined.

## The Inception of Social Darwinism

Most likely, one of the most puzzling aspects of Nazism and capitalism which fomented liberalism raises to the following question: Why did a religion of frugality and self-constraint usher in social Darwinism?

Jackson Lears in his book *No Place of Grace* (1994) traces the roots of American ethnocentrism that led to social Darwinism, which meant the super race of Anglo-Saxons are divinely enthralled to conquest the world. Basically the answer to the question posed above stems from the rise of an anti-modern wave conjoined to the reaction of craft revivals and martial ideals. For wayward puritans, the advance of capitalism was suspected as a pervasive force that will alienate the hard work that defines the good character. In this token, puritans frightened from the liberal market emphasized the needs of stimulating authentic experiences to avoid the negative effects of vice, consumption and alienatory leisure. From the inception of puritanism, and throughout the nineteenth century, puritans struggled against the liberal market simply because of the levels of greed stimulated in humans' heart by the core of its ideology. Originally, religion and capitalism were incompatible in general terms.

As Lears noted,

> "The accommodation between religion and wealth was never complete; nor was it unprecedented. Many minister refused to issue apologetics for social display and material consumption; some actively protested such a practices. And in any case, religions have often enmeshed in the dominant mores of their historical situations." (p. 25)

However, things are not so easy as they appear. The problem of America as it was formulated by the antimodernists consisted of over-civilization, which means the expansion and application of oppressive rules for workers in favor of capital-owners. As a result of this, exegetes of antimodernism proclaimed the return to an idealized medieval age, where farmers and warriors coexisted in peace:

> "The activist version of anti-modernism preached regeneration through preindustrial craftsmanship and pastoral simple life, or posed the violent lives of medieval warriors as a refreshing contrast to the blandness of comfort." (p. 57)

Undoubtedly, this paves the way for the advance of a new unknown trend, which echoed the medieval pastime and the chivalry of the founding Anglo-Saxon warriors, to revere the tendency of the bourgeois to relax and their appetite for money. Only the force which is enrooted in the blood of Anglo Saxons will fight against the threatening vices produced by capitalism. In so doing, the world not only should be emulated the Anglo-Race, but also it adjoined to long-simmering ideas of anti-Semitism. In Europe, the chivalry of Anglo-warriors as a vital force of renovation found in Nazism its most sadist expression, while in the United States it helped the WASP elite to construct barriers not only to exclude ethnicities (considered by them as inferior) but also to keep blacks under control. With the passing of years, this climate of racism coupled to the needs of adopting businesses and profits maximization as real sign of superiority of whites over other races. In a subtler version, antimodernist writers not only legitimized ideologically the free market they had originally decided to fight, but also posed in America a pretext to expand the most successful civilization, the only one where democracy melded different races into an efficient machine of production, to the rest of the world. In other terms antimodernism was ideologically the tenet to forge American imperialism.

One of the most fervent supporters of this ideology, Frank Norris, alerted that two drives will lead America to the top of nations: one is associated to warfare, the other, to businesses. The archetype of the Middle Ages provided to Norris the grounding race impulse whose rage and bravery had no comparison.

"The Anglo-Saxon activism of the 1890s, coupled with Norris' psychic need to embrace a conventional manliness, led him to shift the martial ideal from past to present. Seeking an identity outside bourgeois society he found its values difficult to escape. His antimodern impulse led not to dissent or even nostalgia but to the revitalization and transformation of modern culture. Beginning in a romantic medievalism, Norris ended by affirming modern imperialism." (Lears, 1994, p. 132)

Americans and Europeans felt a certain distrust of materialism and opted to return to a biased landscape of medieval chivalry to reinforce their own irrationality. The struggle with Others gave them a privileged position as exemplary race, while fascination for aggressive impulses created internally a climate of Darwinism where the stronger eats the weaker. This worship of force strengthened a dormant sentiment of anti-Semitism on both sides of Atlantic. As Lears put it,

"Yet this antimodern quest for authenticity is not reducible to either the raptures of military men or the slogans of contemporary self-help manuals; it resisted as well as reinforced the modern obsession with personal fulfillment." (p. 138)

Indeed, this obsession to return to "primordial times," to show Americans are part of selected or chosen peoples, reminds us not only how individualism pervasively invaded their culture, but also of their struggle with Others to achieve individual goals. However, here two objections should be made to Lears's argument. Firstly, the suffering of these men had nothing to do with the narcissism of death-seekers we have discussed in this book. Basically, farmers and workers in the middle of the nineteenth or the start of the twentieth century were characterized by the acceptance of sacrifice and suffering as a sign of stronghold (Lears, 1994). As these Anglo-warriors who supposedly, stories said, conquered Europe, modern workers avoided any type of sensual pleasure to work hard for their community.

## Hitler, Superman and Eugenics in America

In postmodern America, the struggle for Others set the pace to an extreme individualism where the suffering of Others gives the self happiness and satisfaction. At some extent, the crisis of authority puritanism was unable to resolve started a new stage where competition and conquest replaced the original values of charity and assistance. The configuration of an Anglo-elite doubtless, even after the WWII, preserved the social Darwinism in the core of America, which meant that Hitler and his sadist crimes, even defeated, passed to the United States in the figure of cultural entertainment. Not only did the American cinema center its attention on the evils of Nazi Germany, the limitations of intolerance and dictatorship, but also it posed democracy and capitalism as the best of possible worlds. In this process, America became an empire to the extent that Superman and other superheroes such as Batman and Wonder Woman embodied the Nazi ideals of a "super-race" whose destiny was originally to conquest humankind. Americans went far in constructing the same ideology but in a more nuanced way than had the Germans. We, the smarter and stronger super-men, are needed to export our greatest democracy to the world. Emeritus Professor from SUNY at Buffalo, Geoffrey Skoll, said that

> "Catastrophes occur when systemic regulators no longer contain the conflict through various institutional responses. Such a crisis always holds the potential for bifurcation of the system. Bifurcation occurs at a tipping point where the system stops organizing itself and enter in a chaotic state." (Skoll, 2010, p. 28)

The elite's reaction in times of crisis seems not to be persistent with their own interests. Aristocrats do not try to save the system and its functioning well, which paradoxically facilitated the collapse. Egocentrism coupled with individual interests and a wider sentiment of fear, are at a first stage, a big problem for the involved societies and a sentence of death. Comparable with the Roman Empire's and feudal disintegration, late-capitalism's crisis seems to recur to military-machine expansion to keep the control and trade but unlike these past empires, in our modern times the nation-state is inextricably interconnected. As a result of this, the collapse may be very well more apocalyptic than in other times. The reliance on fear works as a conduit for status-quo and elites to maintain their privileges.

Throughout the existent economic crisis, Skoll adds, 9/11 can be equaled to the Reichstag Fire in 1933, where leaders imposed the need for a preventive attack (against communists) and even beyond the boundaries of Germany. To some extent, the United States took advantage of the tragedy that represented the World Trade Center.

> "Regardless of questions about the origins, causes, or perpetrators of the attacks, 9/11 marked a turning point in the history of the world, because the political and economic leadership took advantage of the opportunity of Bush had identified. At this point, and may be forever, their precise thoughts, plans and strategies remain hidden." (p. 35)

Following this reasoning, the consequent interventions in Middle East follow significant lines based on "military action" to achieve dominance in strategic zones, mass support in metropolitan towns, and extraction of local resources or surplus from conquered countries. Undoubtedly, for Skoll the policy of fear conducted by the United States and its war on terror is the result of a planned campaign conducted by the ruling classes in times of uncertainty. Of course, whenever these classes feel under attack or in danger, fear allows two important things. The most important is the internal indoctrination that gives sense to a shared territory and culture, but secondly fear revitalizes consumerism by trivializing the critique.

Why did the Anglo-world support the US preventive war on terror?, the coincidences? Skoll brilliantly said Canada, Australia and the United Kingdom not only share similar cultural background with the United States, they represent an exclusive club of rich countries that resist slumping down. This sentiment of terror paves the ways for the advent of dictatorship simply because it gradually modifies the rights of people, the constitution and the legal framework that assures the principle of civility. Skoll's deep gaze examines slippery matters as torture, fear, local-crime aversion, modernity, evolution and state and the end of liberty in a fluid and all-encompassing way. With this book, one starts to understand the events that characterized US international strategies in recent years. Discussing this in depth, the function of state is to maintain the equilibrium by exerting power and violence over its population. In times of low conflict, the legitimacy of the state rests on the market, which confers to the system a certain stability. Nonetheless, in the context of chaos and disorder the state resorts to violence to refashion the lost order. Similarly, the market mediates among human beings by imposing a state of gratification in lieu of constraints, but the moment the control weakens, fear seems to be the last attempt to recover legitimacy. Skoll goes on to acknowledge that

> "Fascism exercises social control through deprivation, identification with a powerful leader, and aggression against internal and external enemies. Liberal capitalism replaces denial with indulgent consumerism and lifestyles replace status identifies such a race." (p. 45)

After the attacks to New York in 2001, these subtle forms described in the earlier paragraph set the pace for the logic of fascism. As previously explained, Skoll argues that fascisms (and Stalinism) were certainly constructed under the logic of emergency. These policies permit taking control suppressing elementary rights. Rather, the hegemony of the liberal mind is associated with consensus and not violence. If hegemonic control is based on two forms, alliances with neighbours and violence, the United States took the monopoly of capital, expanding loans to other developing countries by means of international organisms such as the World Bank and the International Monetary Fund. The economic dependence of peripheral countries was indeed counterproductive for the United States for many reasons. The first attempt to articulate a systematic expansion was the issuance based on interest that created a huge debt, and secondly, a growing sentiment of resentment of the third world since these loans aggravated US situations. The globalized capital engendered for the liberal state a special form of obedience that, in contrast with other authoritarian republics, shaped a specific conscious-ness centered on calculation, cultural consumption and rationale. The policies of terror are the necessary result for US expansion that led involuntarily to the cur-rent crisis. While authoritarian regimes suppress the dissent, liberal hegemonies marginalize it. That way, one of the main contributions of Skoll to politic fields is linked to the need of reconsider the roots of democracy and dictatorship and rethink under what context a supposed democratic country can trespass the boundaries of autocracy (the power of only-one) and of course the pervasive role of fear in such a process. Trauma can alter the reality of self, and 09/11 changed forever US policy respecting international affairs. This begs a more than interesting question: Is America a fascist nation?

## Democracy and Totalitarianism

In his recent book *Artist of the Possible* Matt Grossman (2014) understands that the United States is an empire, and this wakes up sentiments of hate and support at the same time. The moot point Grossman explains is that American insularity had some limitations for policy-makers to dialogue with citizenry beyond the bureaucracy of institutions. In this respect, democracy was seen as a process of political decentralization and autonomy of powers, which should lead to an atomization of different agents and institutions, all of them without an all-encompassing political power to impose their voices over others'. In that way, each side should negotiate with others when proposing new campaigns or any type of radical change in policies.

> "[*Artist of the Possible*] challenges Americans' view of democratic government. Despite Abraham Lincoln's vision that our government is of the people, by the people and for people, there is little evidence that the most important outcomes of the policy process follow uniformly from the opinion of American public of their expressions in elections. Instead, these inputs matter for policymaking only alongside factors like research and interest group lobbying, each under a limited set of circumstances. Policymakers can and do collectively ignore public opinion and the direction of elections result, sometimes by enacting contrary policy but most often by making no change at all." (Grossman, 2014, p. 9)

Though this system evinced some limitations since it took a conservative spirit, Grossman adds, the main goals of democracy were oriented to prevent any person or party from concentrating too much power to subjugate the rest. This system, which paradoxically was based on the need to protect the interest of the status quo, crystalized after 1945 with the end of WWII. The preliminary chapters of *Artist of the Possible* discuss the best methodological options to study policy-makers as a net as well as the necessary sources of information used in the research. Grossman acknowledges that one of the conceptual limitations of the specialized literature consists in a lack of understanding how policies are formulated, negotiated and achieved. In so doing, he criticized the four most-used theories in political science today: *Agenda Setting, Macro Politics, Issue Typologies and Actor Success* models). At a first glance, Agenda Setting seems to be oriented to explore the role of media as meaning producers that sooner or later determine the understanding of citizenry. As noted, American democracy was cemented on a complex multilayered system where many agents exert counterbalanced pressure to avoid media populism. Rather, the second family of theories, the Macro Politics model, emphasizes the government's ideological control that sanctions laws to protect its interests. From the intersection of election results, ideologies and public opinion, a much wider agreement surfaces. The third model, Issue Typologies, aims at the role played by social change resulting from the temporal consensus reached in some areas of politics while others are left behind. Last but not least, the model of Actor Success sets forward a conceptual corpus which understands that the influence exerted by some actors depend on their probabilities of success.

Centering his content on analysis in almost 790 policy enactments since 1945, Grossmann combines an accurate diagnosis of the policy-making process with other sources which range from social network analysis to the comparison with public laws and other secondary sorts of documents. The main thesis of this work is that entrepreneurs and proponents of change face serious barriers for accessing the rights local voices are asking for. The different institutions and actors not only prevent policy change but also advocate that little policy change be granted. In a decentralized system where checks and balances cause disadvantaging effects, not surprisingly, governments should overcome many obstacles to echo popular demand. This point is brilliantly addressed throughout Grossman's Chapter 3.

From 1961 to 1976, the US federal government enacted numerous policies in its favor to strengthen not only its power before the other legislative powers but also a new governing network that faced serious political instability resulting from the advance of uncontrolled changes. Rather than achieving a system sensible to popular claims, it became what political scientists call a *"long great society."* This period was characterized not only by prolific policy-making enactments, but also by the convergence of presidents, group interests and entrepreneurs to legislate for peoples. Influenced by a liberal spirit, the long great society was a result of the convergence of political coalitions, which, beyond any ideology, embraced a point of agreement. Neither media nor ideology exerts influence in the Long Great Society's inception. Grossman's argument reviews the disparity of actors as well as the orchestration of interests sometimes leads toward the failures in policy change. The paradox lies in that while at the micro level, American democracy encourages individual entrepreneurship, at the macro level it goes in the opposite direction. The current theory of American policy-making shows some limitations to precisely the impact of media on real politics. And this happens because it was constructed on a status quo bias, Grossmann concludes. Though the Madisonian model is successful in limiting social change instilled by governmental policy-making, which benefits the balance among powers, it runs the costs of limiting popular expression. Not only fascinating but pungent in its argument, *Artists of the Possible* exhibits a solid argument regarding the ebbs and flows of American administrations as well as sheds light on how ruling elites have historically monopolized political stability by the adoption of a decentralized system. This book invites readers to reconsider the core of democracy, or, in terms of Grossman American democracy, poses the criticism in what I've dubbed "Anglo-Democracy," which means the dissociation of citizens and their representatives, creating a gap which is fulfilled by business corporations. As originally coined in ancient Greece, democracy comes from an old resource known as *demos* which was used by lay-citizens to invoke an assembly whenever a passed law was considered unjust. However, neither the authority of king nor senate was renovated by elections. Instead, Anglo-democracy is a capitalist construal to forget old *demos*-posing elections and self-representation as primary cultural values. While relegating Others as the right of laypeople to derogate laws that affect their interests, Anglo democracy facilitates homogenizing large groups of the population that otherwise never would be standardized into the same ethnicity. As a result of this, Anglo democracy, which conjoined to the expansion of capitalism, served as a disciplinary mechanism of control conducive to the hegemony of the nation-state (Korstanje, 2015).

Returning to Skoll, not surprisingly some social scientists developed their theories on the basis of emotional speculation instead of real and accurate diagnoses. It is tempting to say, for some left-wing scholars, democracy and the nation-state serve as a shelter before the rise and consequent invasion of the free market into all spheres of life. Instead of this, Skoll reminds us of the importance to revisit these ideals, since the nation-state and capitalism are inextricably entwined.

In view of that, the widespread belief that the capitalist system reproduces through the growth of inequality and poverty is not new, since it has been discussed widely by Marxists and post-Marxists in the four corners of the world. However, the intersection of terrorism and capitalism seems be a heated discussion which today retains considerable concern from scholarship. We are told that working is the best project in how we can spend our time, whereas terrorism is an act of hatred-filled hearts or maniacs. But to what extent is this true?

In *Globalization of American Fear Culture*, Geoff Skoll (2016) continues a much deeper discussion instilled by former work, *Social Theory of Fear* (2010). At a closer look, the act of governing through fear is used by the United States to create a culture of mistrust. From the onset, the United States was based on the belief that the world was a dangerous place to live. Over recent decades in the twentieth century, fear was used to enhance the legitimacy of the elite, sometimes oriented for the workforce to accept policies that otherwise would be rejected. At the time capital and the American empire expanded to colonize new worlds, a much deeper sentiment of fear accompanied the politics. Therefore, it is safe to say we live in a world characterized by a "global fear" which is functional to a particular way of making politics. One of the aspects that facilitated the expansion of capitalism was the idea that citizens live in the best of all possible worlds. Beyond the boundaries of consuming society, of course, any change represents a threat for popular parlance, a barrier to overcome. In the first chapter of *Globalization of American Fear Culture*, Skoll traces the historical roots of the culture of fear in America. In retrospect, the capitalist system and theories of economy showed widely that accumulation is feasible only if we introduce exploitation as a key factor to produce and distribute wealth into a few hands. The monopolization of surplus value, as Marx puts it, resulted not only from human creativity but also by the means of the elite to commoditize labor into exchangeable goods. The number of rank-and-file workers involved in a process of production affects directly the profits of capital owners. From that moment on, the capital reproduction seems to be always to the detriment of the workforce. In this mayhem, whenever conflict arises, fear undermines the possibility for claimers and protesters to impose their views. Two major instruments were used by the privileged classes to maintain their control, ideology and repression. While the latter appealed to surveillance to exert violence against the pathological agents, the former one was enrooted in a process of fear-mongering that limited the negotiation of worker unions. After 9/11, total forms of control were established in private life, subordinating individual rights to the collective well-being, which means a more secure society. Leisure industries were witness to obstructive methods of surveillance over lay citizens. It was unfortunate that this trend makes from the United States a fascist state. In this introductory section, the author combines his erudition by pitting historical cases where governments used fear in their favor against the United States and its Anglo-allies in the war on terror. In the second chapter, Skoll discusses to what extent the elite in America devoted its resources to forge a culture of fear which passed from communism toward terrorism. The organization of labor conjoined to profit maximization are two key factors behind the manipulation of fear. Though the actors changed, the dynamic is the same. Doubtless, this is one of the merits place Geoffrey Skoll now is a must-read author on terrorism issues. From its inception, the United States was always an imperialist power which struggled in four major events: the *Philippine War, Korean War, Cold War* and *Vietnam War*. Though the two total world wars involved the United States as well, no less true is that in these events the United States played the role of an empire inspiring a model that situates it as the "administrator" of capitalism. The management of exploitation centers on a genocidal campaign to discipline communists. The problems of identity and liberal consumerism are placed under the lens of critical scrutiny. The period 1968–1973 not only encouraged a liberalization of human relationship, it induced substantial changes in economies worldwide. During this age the spin doctors of capitalism precaritized the power of workers, paving the pathway for the rise of neoliberalism during the 1990s. Against this backdrop, the expansion of the United States as the unique imperial power was possible after the collapse of the Soviet Union, but without the legacy of the United Kingdom in financial leadership, it would have never taken place. A mantle passed from one power to the other as the United States became the center of manufacture and trade. The globalization of fear is assessed in Grossman's Chapters 6, 7 and 8. The direct intervention and full-scale wars are ideologically legitimized by the need to bring to Others the ideals of American democracy, liberty, freedom and mobility. However, at the bottom, this globalized culture of fear hides dark interests associated with exploitation. Paradoxically, these types of interventions suggest that terrorism needs the use of force, but in so doing, impotence and deprivation surface.

To set an example, Skoll adds, while the United States, supported by financial investors, the IMF or NGOs, arrives at the Middle East to take the local politics on its hands, a state of chaos and political instability dominates the environment. The allegory of war on terror leads governments not to tackle real dangers produced by capitalism such as pollution or global warming. Unless otherwise resolved, the question of whether the United States and its domains pay attention to terrorism as the main threat of the West, surpassing other more terrible risks, one imagines that the probabilities our civilization collapses are higher than previously thought. Anyway, citizens are prone to develop sustainable practices of consumption that encourage a real democracy from the bottom to the top.

After further review, I feel Professor Skoll presents a well-argumented book which is the result of years of academic maturation and research. Starting from the premise that post-Marxian studies have a lot to say on terrorism issues, most of them discriminated by the academy, Skoll exerts a radical and illustrative criticism on the "culture of fear" in the United States. It gives us an impressive snapshot of America so that readers may expand their understanding of what capitalism is. To my mind, this is one of those books that are a must-read reference,

In future approaches, Skoll should resolve what I dubbed as the "Hobbesian dilemma of politics," which means that Marxism was wrong with respect to the role of power in societal fabric (appproaching an argument closer to Weber's). To put this in bluntly, with Thomas Hobbes we learned that fear underlies the world of politics even during democracy. Although economic production plays a vital role in the formation of society, it is not a determinant. There is nothing like a progress toward an end of class struggle, which advances through history. This suggests that society is not affected by fear, but that society itself results from the imposition of mechanisms oriented to discipline fear. In other terms, society is created by the fear. The problem with wayward puritans lies in the fact that they developed a cosmology of conflict where sublimation was affordable only by the imposition of sacrifice. The sense of predestination closed their future in order for the Anglo-worker to demonstrate he or she deserves salvation. In this stage, social Darwinism did the rest. Capitalism worked not only through the culture of fear or consumption imposed on citizens, but also by the fact that they enter in competition with others with an exaggerated idea about their real probabilities of success. Because Americans feel special, superior or even supermen, narcissism undermines the social trust. The survival of the strongest is the final goal, but behind this, only one is the winner. We can see scenes of this nature in main reality shows such as *Big Brother* or even in films such as *The Hunger Games*, where the glory of the few entails the ruin of the rest. This is an ideological resource to normalize the precaritization of the workforce. Inevitably, the war of all against all emulated by Darwinism allows the reproduction of material asymmetries by means of which capitalism expands. The question of whether capitalism produces advances in health, which often saves lives while at the same time expands death and fear everywhere, is unresolved in Skoll's argument, but very well invites the discussion of the next section.

## Capitalism and the Production of Life

To fulfill the need to impose the so-called supremacy of white Anglo-Saxons over other cultures represented in the United States, the cradle of capitalism, an attempt was made to separate other races which were considered inferior. Let's remind readers that a whole portion of intelligentsia in Europe as well as social Darwinism rested on the belief that evolution should be figured into the rhythm of a unilineal growth which marked the difference between civilized and uncivilized cultures. Those who had the luck of being inserted into trade and travels had the opportunity to develop more efficient adaptive forms than did others (Anderson & Grove, 1989; Degler, 1991; Hawkins, 1997; Hofstadter, 1992 [1944]; McClintock, 2013). In the seminal book *Iron Cage*, Ronald Takaki (1990) explored how racism was pervasively used as a mechanism of control form the inception of the United States. In the founding parents of America as Benjamin Franklin and Thomas Jefferson, the concerns for the future was associated to the needs of civilizing this non-European others, but at the same time, they doubted on the cultural disposition of aborigines and blacks to be incorporated to a "great society." Medicine and legal medicine played a vital role in configuring the barriers for these non-Westerners to be psychically isolated in ghettos, reservoirs and camps. As Takaki brilliantly revealed, the first essays of psychiatry shed the light on the perverse nature of aborigines as well as their lack of disposition to industrial labor. Labeled and stereotyped as "weary, idle, ugly and lazy," these non-European others were legally excluded in the formation of the nation. In this process, the medical gaze worked ideology not only to stress the supremacy of Anglo-race over other collectives, and ethnicities, but planned to extirpate "blacks" from the bowels of the capitalist system (Takaki, 1990). This suggests that the consolidation of medicine as a professional career and the genealogy of racism were inevitably entwined. Paradoxically, the cultural project of capitalism was originally oriented to expand lives, while producing death in those Others who do not look like me. At a closer look, the tension between an atmosphere of liberty which pitted colonists against England, was incompatible with racism. It woke up many anxieties in the writers and politicians because slavery represented one of the main threats for Republicanism. In order for preventing the migration of new blacks to the land of "lovely whites," republicanism nourished a paternalist discourse that was aimed at finding a new land for these "undesired guests" (Takaki, 1990). This means that American culture evolved under a recalcitrant racism which served to reduce the original puritan anxieties respecting to the "otherness." Hereafter, the production of life in capitalism was based on serious material asymmetries, which were never shortened.

Given this argument, unlike Nazi Germany America truthfully adopted new ethnicities coming from forced migratory fluxes who were symbolically re-educated into the mainstream cultural values of civilization, trade, liberty and achievements. If the hopes of founding parents were associated with the creation of a "special society," there were some elements which not only contradicted this ideal, but also represented a problem for Anglo-whites. In this vein, Takaki says,

> "The black and the Indians, as they existed in Jefferson's imagination and in the political economy of America, had been separated from each other. Jefferson viewed each of them as a different problem. Consulting sources of violence and sexuality, the black was a growing and threatening blot, to be removed to Africa. Close to nature and without government, the Indian was an obstacle to be removed to the West or to be incorporated as Lockean property-owning farmer and become a part of ourselves." (Takaki, pp. 63–64)

The different treatment depended not only on the value each ethnicity placed on the capitalist system; for example, while blacks were exploited as cheaper manpower, the same cannot be applied to Native Americans who manifested a reluctant attitude toward labour. The former were incorporated to be systematically exploited while the latter grew with full autonomy but in pauperism and poverty. After all, both ethnicities were excluded from the promises of Uncle Sam to the extent they would wait a very long time before their rights were recognized. Given these conditions, the doctrine of wealth and capitalist accumulation evinced inequalities among classes and races that reinforced the puritan influence in the Republic. While racism is imposed, the medical-gaze constructs legally and symbolically the necessary platform for ethnicities to be subordinated to the whites and their ethnocentric discourse. This raises the pungent question: Where does the origin of social Darwinism start?

An historical review of medical-gaze evinces that biology played a vital role in configuring the basis for the inception and evolution of supermen, who are a new class of citizens oriented to consume what potentiated their strengths, skills and intelligence. Not surprisingly, pills to raise the IQ as well as advances to improve genetics are in the United States a fertile source for the production of a "superman" who continues the dreams of Nazis. Not only is this a result of narcissism as it was discussed in the introductory chapter, but also it is from the same cultural project which accelerated after WWII.

In this manner, Paul Starr (1982) detailed the transformation of American medicine as a sovereign profession in making a vast and profitable industry. Medicine and medical discourse not only monopolized the authority of the professional class healing the disease of people but also allowed the construction of hospital infrastructures to replicate the codes, rituals, rules and authorities of doctors in the rest of society. While the technological advances during the twentieth century prompted the fabrication of faster cars, which accelerated travel and other geographical movements among citizens, physicians organized the core of the productive system. The certificates issued by doctors not only were used to indicate those workers who were too mentally ill for working but also endorsed a license to others who needed social care and protection. This means that capitalism seems to be based on two similar constructs: hotels that connected the geographies of distant cities in hours, and hospitals that nourished the discourse around of what should be an ideal worker (Starr, 1982).

The construction of roads, adjoined to the advance in mobile technologies during the nineteenth century, reduced the time of travels for doctors who were accustomed or forced to attend patients at home. It resulted not only in a substantial reduction of medicine costs, but buttressed doctors to earn more money for their services. If anything was clear, it was that the high cost of travel was the key factor in the individualism and isolation of the medical gaze. Once Americans migrated to live in urban cities, medicine surfaced as a professional discipline as well as the authoritative voice in the question of life and death. Basically, the rise of cities coupled to travel revolution generated a fluid communication which pushed down the costs of medicine. The second entry in this discussion consisted of the multiplication of hospitals to treat sickness. The treatment and care which was reserved for women and wives at home, now passed to the hegemony of nurseries and doctors who monopolized knowledge to save the lives of citizens.

> The boundaries defining medical profession might have been drawn on any of three lines: graduates versus no graduates of medical schools; members versos nonmembers of medical societies; licensed versos non licensed practitioners. None of these worked … only graduates could be a licensed and only a licensed could practice. All licensed physicians, would have strong inducements to join their local medical society." (Starr, 1982, p. 46)

From that moment on, the triumph of medical reason not only contributed to the production of new medicines and the elaborations of substances (drugs) in the pharmaceutic industry, but also seriously expanded the boundaries of life, endowing the layman with special attributes, skills and powers to become a superhero. Virilio (2010) seems not to be wrong when he says the revolution in mobilities not only brought further free time, which was fulfilled by visual allegories that trapped the autonomy of the modern consumer, but also eroded the basis of scientific inquiry to be at the disposal of the market. Unless otherwise resolved, medicine now heals workers only for them to be working on.

Today people do not consume other things than pills that potentiate their skills. It is interesting to see how celebrities, actors and politicians give their testimonies after tasting *the brain plus IQ* which substantially improves intelligence and provides them with advanced brain functions. Plenty of drugs are at disposal of an ever-growing demand of people who want to feel different with respect to "the mediocre Other." For this reason, laypeople not only have developed an uncanny crave for being smartest, strongest and fastest, they also want to be godlike. Originally, Paul Virilio (2010) anticipated the compliance of the market with science in his book *The University of Disaster*. As already discussed in Virilio's account, greater business corporations used biology to maximize their profit-oriented goals instead of to protect citizens. However, as Starr warned, the professionalization of medicine opens the doors for a paradoxical situation. Pitted against their colleagues to get a better job, doctors and practitioners entered into a platform of competition where all will struggle against all only to survive. Although the affiliation to medical associations places medicine in the throne of selected disciplines and discounted alternative wisdoms, no less true is that industrialization leads to an atmosphere of extreme competition among professionalized doctors to gain more patients. While medicine was professionalized, sickness became in an institution.

Given the above argument, it is tempting to question the role played by science in the configuration of a society which positions competition over other cultural values. This moot point will be addressed in the following section.

## The Role of Science in This Modern World

Two scholars who have critiqued the role of tourism as an entertainment industry were Paul Virilio and Marc Augé. This section analyzes their contributions to the theme, and uses that analysis to also show why tourism can be conceived as a way of avoiding real travel, or in other terms, an ideology that leads to nowhere. Paul Virilio dichotomizes the world into the real and the unreal. He proposes that the technologically led advance has created a contradictory situation. On one hand, it allows us to rapidly cover great physical distances, connecting people throughout the globe, but on the other, technology is alienating people in a biased reality. Recognizing that we human beings have developed a natural ability to communicate our feelings to achieve adaptation to the environment, Virilio says that the communication media encompass dispersed events in diverse geographical points. This information complex occludes the subjectivity of personhood and instead channels it into mass consumption. What today we watch on TV is not reality, but a biased image of nothing. This fictional dream serves as disciplinary limits to the self. The means of transport, faster than in other times, resulted in an unabated acceleration that never stops. As a result of this, social trust not only has declined, but also has been commoditized in the emptiness of space. If the excess of velocity is accompanied by a sentiment of inferiority, repressed in the social imaginary, Virilio adds, it creates a false consciousness where human beings believe they control death and life. The thesis of Virilio is simple beyond his rhetoric: The acceleration of mobile technology has created much more free time. This time is fulfilled by a false ideology where spatiality is ended. The advent of motor vehicles allowed substantial improvement in the forms by which people travelled as well as giving them more time, changing the boundaries between "here" and "there." The virtualization of reality upends the boundaries between reasons and effects. The events broadcasted by media are interposed one by one all the time. Paradoxically, travels are possible when the Other is accepted alone. Therefore, international tourism that neglects the presence of the Other is the expression of moving to nowhere. In this context, Virilio contends that international tourism revitalizes the ancient colonial violence that characterized the nineteenth century.

Building isolated resorts and "Club-Meds" function as fortresses in a desert. Symbolically, Virilio refers to the desert as a state of emotional desolation. It is important not to lose sight of the fact that Virilio argues that tourism is a hegemonic instrument to create financial dependence and submission from the periphery to the center (Virilio, 1996; 2007).

In a similarly minded line, Augé, in his work *Places and Non-Places* (1995), says that tourism mythologizes displacement only under commoditized forms of consumption where the human bond is fictionalized. Travelers, indeed, are not interested in the well-being of others, except to encounter special experiences that feed their own egos. Tour operators, from his viewpoint, divide the map, creating new circuits emulating a confabulated tale, where natives are domesticated under the rubric of the good savage. Tourism represents "impossible travel" where discovery sets the pace to conformity (Augé, 1995).

The question of authenticity was also analyzed by Dean MacCannell. Starting from the premise that aborigines identify themselves with a certain totem, MacCannell argues that modern citizens have certainly made of consumerism a symbolic pattern of cultural identification. Following Lévi-Strauss's contributions, MacCannell argues that Karl Marx was the first scholar who started with the tradition of understanding how social structures interact with agents. For Marx, society projects an ideal image of everything that can produce deprivation and suffering. Daily, human being's desires and unmet needs are sublimated as a form of religion and ideology. These types of staged-paradises are often fabricated by aristocracies to maintain their authority and legitimacy over the populace. In a similar manner, tourism serves as a dreamlike mechanism geared to provide modern workers an interval of happiness and relaxation in order for them to be reinserted into production chains. Following a Marxian development, MacCannell avows that tourist experience is comprised of three parts: (1) a front-stage wherein stakeholders portray a sightseeing depiction elaborated for an audience (model), (2) subjective emotions which are triggered by the experience once people are at their destinations (influence), and ultimately (3) the agent who acts as an intermediary by gathering the synergy of the two aforementioned elements. Are tourists attracted by the misfortune of otherness—poverty, disease, and so on? In his treatment of the relationship between poverty and attractiveness, MacCannell suggests that modern tourists are not characterized by their sensibility to suffering, but by curiosity and cynicism. The quest for difference becomes pivotal in understanding modern mobility and mass tourism (MacCannell, 2003).

In *The University of Disaster*, Virilio (2010) claims that in the past, geography remained immutable before disasters and impermeable to tragic issues. The advance of science moved at a snail's pace by prioritizing the quality of knowledge. Its objectivity lies in the observation of facts rooted in reality. However, things have changed a lot. The digital world has blurred time, prompting science to study thousands of simultaneous events, which does not lead to any coherent logic. The mobile industries of tourism and insurance are progressively eroding the barriers of the city. The market system obliterated the sense of place. The importance of risk is not determined by its effects, but by its substance. Everything that is important in this world cannot be acquired without loss of substance. This means that there is no real knowledge without risk. Reducing major risks to zero, as modern science attempts to do, is not only a serious error but also a way of obscuring the truth. Virilio warns that the problems are not risks but "the desert of the mind" inherited in "turbo-capitalism." If human beings do not change their values by introducing ethics, the problem of climate change will be aggravated with the passing of decades. Ironically, globalized capital is not willing to change its current ways of production and pollution. Rather, experts and universities are called on by insurance corporations and banks to predict the effects of the next disasters (Klein, 2007). Applied research serves the interests of the market. Any attempt to mitigate the greenhouse effect is not aimed at tackling the problem of air pollution. While only the superfluous aspects of global warming are considered by the financial center, the underlying values of globalized capital that generated the problem remain. Paradoxically, while we constructed a new economic system that valorized life, the available technology is unable to predict disasters unless they affect an individual's property. This means that the natural asymmetries of capitalism between capital owners and workers, the rich and the poor or haves and have-nots, far from being closed, has been enlarged in view of a new biology where competence preceded protection. At some extent, bio-capitalism is oriented to potentiate workers only to compete with others, not to defy the status quo. Concepts such as intelligence, creativity a sensibility are only accepted and channeled into hard work. This represents what some specialists dubbed "the rise of bio-capitalism."

## The Rise and Hegemony of Bio-Capitalism

One of authoritative voices in genomic-related research, Kaushik Sunder Rajan introduces the term "biocapital" to gain further understanding on the post genomic World. Centered on the contributions of Michel Foucault and Karl Marx, Rajan understands that the start of biotechnology continues an old, already existent stage of capitalism, where genomics and DNA information became exchangeable commodities handled by upstream and downstream companies. The term "biocapitalism" is not limited to a new production of life, since Rajan recognizes there are many forms of capitalism(s). The fact is that the science of biology is co-determined by the needs of capital owners, which commoditizes social relations. In the words of the author,

"I wish to clarify the relation of biocapital to capital (and to capitalism) in precisely these terms. Bio capital does not signify a distinct epochal phase of capitalism as we have known it. At the same time, there are significant particularities to biocapital that have to do both with institutional structure within which drug development takes places, and with the techno-scientific changes in the life sciences and biotechnologies over the last thirty years, that make it too simplistic simply to say that biocapital is a case study of capitalism having to do with the life of science... rather, the relationship between capitalism and what I call biocapital is one where the latter is, simultaneously, a continuation, an evolution of, and a form distinct from, the former." (K. S. Rajan, 2007, p. 10)

Methodogically, Rajan faces the challenge to compare datasets in two contrasting marketplaces: the United States and India. While the former is characterized by a great atomization among competitors, India, though emulating the capitalist system, is strongly enrooted in a mixed economy, where capitalism did not flourish with the same power that it did in the United States. His main argument is aimed at discussing how biocapital comprises material forms of production with abstract knowledge, which is produced and co-produced to impose meaning, how life should be interpreted. In other terms, we cannot understand the postgenomic world beyond the values of the market that regulates it, as well as the conceptual framework legitimized by modern science. Without any type of objectivity, these values are legally framed by capital owners who map technological advances in favor of their own interests. To set an example, and likely following the puritan logic, in America "the discourse of biocapital" was ushered under the logic of salvation which led to nationalist rhetoric. Basically, the promises of biocapital not only took an individualist perspective, they alluded to a salvationist spirit which contrasted sharply what had happened in India. The needs of innovation, competition and information centrality were the three pillars that marked the arrival and pace of bio-technology in America. The produced knowledge is monopolized and stored by private companies which struggle with others for the control of the market. Following this argument, the power of bio-capitalism centers on the legal force that allows the expropriation of genetic information, dissociating individual from collective rights. Even, it is interesting to discuss the case Moore vs. the Regents of the University of California, where a patient afflicted with leukemia issued a lawsuit against this prestigious educational establishment for the manipulation and patent of his cell line. The supreme court of California denied Moore's claim to access profits of the researcher's invention. Most certainly Moore was deprived of the rights produced by scientists with the exploitation of his own body.

As per the previous argument given, information is the key element for capital investors to appropriate from genomic structure. In other terms, as Rajan wrote,

"The information that is generated from this material is often converted into databases. Those databases (or so it hoped y the companies developing them) the precursors of therapy. In an ideal world, the company that generates the database would hold the information and use in the company's own drug discovery program. In reality, taking drugs to market is so heavily capital intensive that most database companies license their information to big pharmaceutical companies." (p. 61)

While such an expropriation is legally authorized by the state, a tacit ideological discourse points out that science and bioethics play a major role in protecting the lives of citizens, Rajan adds. As legal precedent, Moore vs. California reminds us of the authority conferred by researchers or the net of experts who have the possibility to create new products. Here the sense of creation not only produces value which is exchanged by different stakeholders in a great variety of directions, but they adjoin to a so-called legitimacy through the lens of ethics. Though the discourse is universal in one sense, the monopolization of the United States is in few hands, most of them hosted in the United States. Although biocapital appeals to the construction of a narrative of life, not exactly death, the dynamic seems to be the same. Gift-exchange theory marks the importance of holders who in the circuits of inter-exchange monopolize further unalienable goods (Weiner, 1985; 1992). The biological metaphor situates as one of these valuable goods, which in parallel allows the dissemination of an ideological message to society. This is the point where Rajan starts when confirming the material means of production are co-determined by abstract construal which is socially legitimated. In the development of his argument, there are two clear assumptions. The first and most important, bio-capitalism works in conjunction with risk, which, operating in the future, determines the present time. This creates a new type of ever-waiting consumer who is receptive to the industry of bio-pharmaceutic genetics. Although genetics play a co-determinant role in configuring the existence of self, it triggers "a fetishism of biology" (genomic fetishism):

> "The interpelated subject of genomic fetishism…except in cases otherwise mentioned, is the American who gets foretold his or her probabilities of future health or illness by technology such as a DNA chip. Such a subject, I argue, becomes a patient-in-waiting. But personalized medicine is a bio-capitalist assemblage that demands constant attention to the fact that produced epistemologies and technologies, particularly in the US context, are over-determined as commodities and therefore require a market for their consumption." (K. S. Rajan, 2007, p. 148)

In fact, the contribution of Rajan to the advance in the understanding of thana-capitalism is tangential. He deposits too much attention to the power of risk in the configuration of bio-capitalism. Secondly, this position leaves behind the theory of risk that is any longer explicative of current capitalism. While the nation-state and private sector devote considerable resources to extend life, health of population, or the expectancy of life, no less true is that death is stronger in the social imaginary. This happens by two main reasons. On a closer look, the process of secularization not only questioned but denied the afterlife. In doing this, the social imaginary developed a pejorative view of death. Anymore, death is used as a platform to a better life, but as an end. Our current obsession for death, which was widely debated in earlier chapters, associates with a very profound desire to live forever. Secondly, bio-politics and bio-capital sound as metaphors that help construct a criterion of exclusivity for those who proclaim themselves as the privileged class. The elite, in that way, alludes to the allegories of competence, progress and success in order for the workforce to be atomized, disorganized or unable to coordinate effort to defy the power of status quo. Ideologically, the discourse of evolution and progress, which was exploited by social Darwinism, situates "Anglo-Saxons" as more civilized, smarter and stronger than other cultures. Their superiority is given by historical and cultural backgrounds that mark a deep difference from other nations. In this atmosphere of conflict, the life is idealized as a great career where only few will reach the real success. The death of Others, despite all available medical technology, is considered as a sign of weakness. In recent years, many destinations focusing on dark tourism as the main option flourished. It is not an accident that a new class, death-seekers, has arisen that not only opts for these types of macabre product, but also shows its obsession with Others' death. What underlies this obsession is the terror of being excluded from the privileged class. Metaphorically speaking, once heaven fell, death was commoditized to be consumed by those who want to make on earth a restricted Eden. Whichever the case may be, thana-capitalism, as a new stage of production that continues former ones, has been enrooted in contemporary society once the society of risk faded. Much discussion is needed on the intersection of death-seekers and modern patterns of consumption, but for the moment, we have introduced into the discussion a new point of entry, which merits to be continued. The founding event of this stage was doubtless the attacks to the World Trade Center, which ignited a new era where terror was commoditized by politicians, media and marketing experts. They not only manipulate our emotions, but also understand how fear and hope paralyzes local protests. Paradoxically, while the capitalist world exerts an all-encompassing control of the bodies by means of consumption, rivalry, conflict and riots emerge as counter reactions of laypeople who coordinate efforts to struggle against nobody. In effect, one of the problems of politics now is that movements such as "*indignados*," "*caceroleros*," or any other protesters have not direct or specific goals in their claims. However, this is a deep-seated issue which should be investigated on another occasion.

The current state of inequality which is explained by action of (thana) capitalism comes from the puritan cosmology. The problem of predestination cemented the possibility to escape from the yoke of the future. As Michel Maffesoli observed, capitalism was produced by a future which does not exist in reality but determines in many ways the present behavior. Doubtless, Maffesoli is today one of philosophers who devotes his attention to the return of tragedy in daily life. Although his contributions have shed light on the philosophical insights, less attention was given to the disaster-related studies. My intention, at some extent, is aimed at reviewing the most interesting hypothesis that places Maffesoli as the scholar of disaster.

Our French philosophers are strongly interested in revealing (deciphering) the puzzle of modernity. In his book *L'Instant èternal: le retour du tragiue dans les societes postmodernes*, (*The Return of the Tragedy in Postmodern Societies*),

Maffesoli understands late capitalism (postmodernism) is based on a conception of a closed future. As the tragedy evolves into an atmosphere of predestination, the future for us was diluted forever. This leads people to live in the present with extreme hedonism and intensity. Similarly to a concentration camp, where inmates embrace the cult of achievements, now workers are extremely overexcited by the cult of achievers. These spaces of death, which characterized the destiny of millions of innocent civilians during WWII, were successfully accepted by capitalism today. Whether these camps exhibited a banner saying "*arbeit macht frei*," which means "work sets you free," not surprisingly, one might confess that workers sacrifice their ideal freedom to a real slavery. The same applies for capitalist corporations nowadays.

Ideologically, Maffesolli understands capitalism as a symbolic trap, where always the immanent disaster is coming. Given this, all else will be immaterial if the tragedy will take place someday. Its nature not only is irreversible but also irremediable tragic. It creates a space of encounters where consumption, hedonism and the aesthetics of individualism converge. We should not lose sight that the culture of pleasure, the sentiment of disaster, and the confronting of destiny resulted from the adoption of a new ethics that takes the instant as the primary value.

As the previous argument asserted, the myth of tragedy is aimed not only toward enthralling a mysticism of destructive creation, but also toward a new continuity of life where past and future dilute. In the return of tragedy in postmodern societies, "otherness" serves as a commodity to be exploited by means of the senses. We are prone to visit exotic landscapes, attending to musical parties as "love parades," taking the "Others" as a criterion of attraction. In a world of attractive appearances, where the future brings only destruction, ethics are subject to what experts think of as the best option. The decisions about our future were made beyond our capacities of understanding; the concept of a closed destiny plays a vital role in cementing our postmodern life. To put this in bluntly, the dramatic conception of the world in modern times evinced the quest for happiness, in a paradise where the subject enjoys its properties or merits in life, capitalizing the individual's pleasure and minimizing the costs. This sort of individualism was the hallmark of modernity. However, things have changed a lot. Postmodernism places the life as a collective property, where the "disaster" weights our individualism, by posing the destiny as something unaffordable for humankind. There is nothing in this world to do when disasters hit. Everything is there—predestined by external forces that have a design for us. However, unlike Weber, who envisaged a disenchantment of the world, Maffesoli formulates a new type of re-enchantment of hedonism, or an ethic of the instant as it has been earlier explained in this book review.

Here, we hold the thesis that neither Weber nor neither Maffesoli formulated the concept of predestination with accuracy. Although Weber, who was closer than was Maffesoli in his description of capitalism, was correct in confirming that the Reform introduced a new thinking associated with predestination, he ignored the influence of Norse mythology in the configuration of predestination. It is clear how Protestants embraced achievements to know if they were in the Book of Life, but there is evidence enough in earlier Christendom, for example in Norse myths of persistence of predestination. In earlier studies, I explained that cultures are disciplined forms of battlegrounds and warfare. Not surprisingly, Anglo-American empires built a cosmology according to their founding cultural values. Maffesoli is wrong at time of interpreting the meaning of *moira* as a closed destiny; even in the battleground Greeks have a free choice to live or die. This happens simply because gods (unlike for Germans) were only advisors. The fate of the warrior is never determined by the gods, but what can be achieved now and here. Ancient Greece was never familiar with anything like predestination. Rather, readers of Norse mythology acknowledge that Walkyrias (daughters of Odin/Wodan) were commissioned to pick up the bodies of fallen warriors. They not only knew *the destiny of the warrior* beforehand, which is the basis of predestination, but also presented death as a form of redemption. Being selected by Odin to enter "Valhalla," was for Germans a great honor. Not surprisingly, the Anglo-world from the outset was marked by disaster and predestination. This was the reason simply why detractors of Weber criticized he was not directing his attention to Catholic Holland, which was the epicenter of an early capitalism. Well, Holland was in the condition of fomenting capitalism because of Weber's Norse cultural matrix. At the same time, the propensity of Anglo-societies to advance in scientific knowledge is derived from its concern for future and risk. Unlike Catholic societies, which are based on charity and tradition, Protestantism is particularly concerned by the closed-fate, thus they devote all resources to colonize the future. To cut a long story short, the current postmodern cultures are future-oriented societies (Korstanje, 2014b; Skoll & Korstanje, 2013).

In this discussion, Kaushik Sunder Rajan (2007) misunderstands the intersection between religion and capitalism. Per his viewpoint, capitalism rests on two main institutions, religion and nation. By the stimulation of futurist scenarios, which can modify or co-determine the structure of behavior in the present, capitalism alludes to the metaphor of biology from a salvationary viewpoint, a new change to life. In consequence, the ability to calculate the future stimulates not only enhances profits but also a fictional landscape which is fulfilled by the needs of consuming. In the age of bio-capitalism, the productions of potential waiting inpatients allows medical discourse to manipulate the future to control the present. This is the reason why the risk as a main element in bio-capitalism plays a crucial role through the introduction of contingency and prophesy. Although illustrative, this argument rests on shaky foundations simply because the colonization of the future implies the destruction of risk. As observed in *A Difficult World* (Korstanje, 2015), the culture of English-speaking countries is based on a terrible panic about the future, simply because they are unfamiliar with the predestined crave of God. The use of biotechnology and postgenomic programs are in consonance of the elimination of any risk. The future man is being programmed not to suffer any sickness, and though it is a utopia, the underlying problem lies in the fact that Anglo-Saxons are afraid of the future. From their inception and evolution as commercial empires, Great Britain and the United States devoted efforts in the creation of a zero-risk society. The paradox remains in thinking that future and risk are two sides of the same coin. While the future allows the presence of risk, because the knowledge is not total, the risk only is enrooted in the future, escaping in this way from the hegemony of determinism. However, if the future is totally colonized by the production of supermen, as the film *Gattaca* showed, the world of risk would end forever. Inscribed as a point of cleavage, violence is only exerted to change what others decide for us. In a world where peace and the lack of violence persist, which turns out to be nonhuman, the hegemony of post-genomic programs undermines the dangerous free choice. Here is where the presence of death serves as a sign one has been chosen by God to participate in the competition. Following this, it is not an accident to see how media, cultural entertainment, disseminates news or scenarios where death is the main protagonist. This is oriented to exorcise the self of the possibility to die, giving to the audience a certain happiness before the Others' disgrace. In that way, news of natural disasters, serial killers, fatal accidents or terrorist attacks are preferred to good news by professional journalism. Death is present in many of our social institutions, besides dark tourism, which means the industry that organizes travels to sites of disaster or catastrophe. This book was an original attempt to decipher the complexity of this new stage of capitalism, thana-capitalism, which focused on the end of risks. This does not mean that the sociologists of risks were wrong; they did the correct diagnosis in evincing the frights for future determination. Rather, our argument is that risk society has gone forever, and a new class, death-seekers, has effectively emerged.

# Conclusion

A new theory of capitalism merits a further discussion on the complexity and disparity of perspectives, which oscillates from the world of risk, to the hegemony of medical gaze to produce a revolution in the genome. While we expand our understanding of fact and events, less attention is given to the effects of our discoveries. This was exactly the main concerns of Beck and Giddens when they portrayed the sociology of risk. At some extent, death seems to be changing everything what has been written in the sociology of capitalism by two main reasons. Firstly, the ideological power of death prompted by the process of secularization defined a new post-organic citizen who is adapted to struggle against others in quest of their pleasure-oriented maximization. Secondly, what is more important, Thana-capitalism inscribes in the continuation of social shifts faced by Westerners over recent decades. As stated in several times throughout this book, we have held the thesis, the concept of beautiness as something related to apollonian logic has changed to more morbid ways of consumptions. Lay-People when planning their holidays do not opt for paradisiacal destinations, located in Caribe but in morbid museums or spaces characterized by the presence of mass suffering or death. This means that new practices of tourism allude to the rise of a new society, where death plays a crucial role not only by setting new values associated to social Darwinism or the supremacy of stronger, a legacy of defeated Nazism, but dividing the world between salved and doomed peoples. An abundant set of bibliography focused on the motivations dark-site visitors as a natural drive to understand our being in this world. By means of *"thanaptosis,"* these specialists say overtly, sites or communities obliterated by natural disasters, catastrophes, traumatic stories, or even terrorism may be very well recycled in order for survivors to give a good lesson on what these types of events happen. Although this term was originally coined by Bryant long time ago, it is necessary to conceptualize on the contradictions of life. What modern citizens are prone to others' death, as we have already explained, corresponds with a Darwinist attempt to keep on within the privileged circle of exemplary citizens. The chapters organized in this book, though can be read separately, and are aimed to discussing to what extent dark tourism practices opened the doors or were further indicators of a new society, which was dubbed as "thana-capitalism." At a closer look, death not only is commoditized by tourists who travel toward sites of mass suffering as

New Orleans, Ground Zero or Auschwitz-Birkenau Museum in Poland; rather death is present in many of the current social institutions which ranges from the journalism which today portrays news related to local crime in a daily basis, to realities shows as Big Brother or movies consumed by teenagers as *Hunger Games, or Divergent.* The culture of a catastrophic society that idolatrize death comes from Christianity, not for the reason we have criticized in Slavoj Žižek's book *The Dwarf and the Puppet*, a rough argument that indicates Christ needed from betrayal to become God, but emphasizing on the crucifixion of Christ as a founding events between two contrasting worlds. This symbolic (a-historical event) paved the ways for the rise of the class of victims, and witnesses. Additionally, in the myth of Noah and his ark that was pressed to gather a couple by specie to preserve the life, after the wish of total destruction, one can find the original cultural roots of thana-capitalism. This would be the main reason why cinema and cultural entertainment has done from Noah a celebrity, a worthy person who obeys the wish of a cruel God that shows how the salvation of few should be done over the ruin of the rest. This legitimizes not only the logic of thana-capitalism, where few concentrates huger portion of wealth while a whole society rests on poverty or struggle for survival. Doubtless, capitalism reproduces faster than thought producing serious material asymmetries among classes. One privilege group which reached the power and monopolized the means of production subordinates the rest. In order for, oppressed workforce not to defy the financial elite, some ideological apparatuses are orchestrated to make workers belief that they are or would be part of something special. As Lasch put it, we cannot dissociate the exploration of capitalism without narcissism, which are constituent of pathological forms of adaptations. In thana-capitalism, life is seen as a long trace where participants do their best to reach the final prize. However, on Olympus there is no place for all, and only one can be the winner. Whenever we are sensitive to hearing news of death, visit sites of disaster or are prone to consume others' death, it reveals it is because we need to feel our superiority over others, victims who had not such luck. The morbid happiness that death-seekers feel, when they consume death, is proportional to disaster-led commoditization. The point of divergence between thana-capitalism and the capitalism of risk is given by the appearance of new indicators exhibiting the rise of an incipient consuming class, death-seekers. Some scholars, such as Steven Pinker, who valorizes this world, argues that the modern world has successfully reached a state of stability and peace as never before. This was possible not only by the action of the Enlightenment, but also by a clear decline in the rate of violence. The problem of social bondage and conflict was set in the agenda of sociology and anthropology from their onset. For the founding parents of these disciplines, capitalism (or industrialism) activates an alienatory mechanism which is conducive to controlling the workforce. In view of that, ideology and alienation would be serving as vehicles toward depersonalization. Sooner or later, industrial societies would face what Durkheim called "anomie," which means the decline of social trust. Undoubtedly, from that moment onwards, social scientists credited that capitalism brought negative effects for laypeople such as the rise of conflict, crime and other deviant behaviors. In parallel, the concentration of wealth, post-Marxists claimed, in few hands triggered the discussion on to what extent Hobbesian doctrine determined the war of all against all. Of course, there was not agreement respecting the reasons of violence in our modern global village. This is exactly the point that Steven Pinker departs from. In this respect, he argues convincingly that far from what a whole portion of academy guesses, violence has declined as a result of a combination of trade, conjoined to the adoption of humanist values, democracy and globalization. Based his development on a titanic investigation (which contains more than 700 pages), Pinker sets forward hard evidence to validate the hypothesis that violence and conflict is declining in the world. At some extent, he continues with the debate left by Norbert Elias and his notion of civilization. Like Elias, Pinker acknowledges that there are some flashpoints which may be corrected, but in comparison with other centuries (even the Middle Ages). This decade (in the inception of twenty-first century) seems to be a most peaceful time in humanity's existence. Two major assumptions are of vital importance for us in this review. First and foremost, civilizations expand their hegemony by the imposition of discourses. These narratives are aimed at silencing or embellishing bloody past-time events in forms of heroic epics. Our heroes not only were cruel persons who have killed thousands of other warriors, but also struggled in appalling battlefronts to impose their interests. This is the first point of entry in this discussion because we tend to think current times are more violent than earlier ones, but historical evidence suggests exactly the opposite. Secondly, sometimes statistics are analyzed following a much deeper emotional logic that distorts the outcome. It is not far-fetched to confirm that the twentieth century was a bloody century since two world wars took place in itm but Pinker adds that humankind has witnessed other genocides and slaughters in earlier centuries. This begs a more than pungent question: Why is violence declining?

For Pinker, Hobbes was in the right direction at the time in exploring the roots of plunder. Peoples attack others through fear, pride or eagerness. The goals for fighters are related not only to predation, but also to honor. In the Middle Ages, plunder and conquests posed the only manner of upward mobility in societies where classes do not exist. In perspective, in traditional societies where peasants and warlords are attached to their lands, conflict is the only valid mechanism to expropriate others from their possessions. At the time trade was introduced as a form of negotiation among peoples and officialdoms, violence plummeted. The use of money not only replaces the need for war but also globalizes the exchange of goods, resulting in an efficient way of deterring predation. Over recent years, we have found some civil conflicts in the world that leads readers to question the idea of civil democratic peace. Is democracy effective in its struggle against terrorism?

Far from being a detractor of democracy, Pinker clarifies that "decent governments" (p. 313) are reasonably democratic because they are prone to trade and market-oriented. Being open to globalized economy, foreign investment or liberal trade helps in reducing the conflicts or their severities for peoples. The main thesis of this titanic project is that the ideals of Enlightenment or the Kantian hopes in a universal peace are possible if nation-states adopt democracy as their primary form of government and endorse the values of liberal market. Following this axiom, US-led invasions to Middle East nations such as Iraq or Afghanistan would be considered legitimate preventive acts for a democratic power against undemocratic societies. This decline of violence is not eternal, and it has been experienced in earlier times. The ebbs and flows of civilization reach different levels depending on the sociocultural conditions of societal order. The ten chapters that form this fascinating book propose a liberal vision of the world which places the belief of a more hostile society under the lens of scrutiny.

Personally, I agree this is an impressive work that compiles methodologically vast ranges of studies and samples alternating quantitative with qualitative approaches. I even share with Pinker the belief that violence is in decline. In order to monopolize the means of production, the financial elite needs peace, mobility, tourism, democracy and commodity-exchanges. However, that violence decreased is not good news simply because capitalism has proved to be a machine to create material asymmetries. As Bauman (2013) puts it, the problem of capitalism rests on the belief that few deserve much, while the rest are on the ruin. Almost 90% of produced wealth is concentrated in 2% of the global population. In this and my previous book (Korstanje, 2015) I explained that this postmodern world can be compared to the film *The Hunger Games* or the reality show *Big Brother*. In both settings, participants are dominant precisely because they remain unfamiliar with the real probability of failing. These competitions, like in the liberal market, are based on the premise of social Darwinism that proclaims "the survival of strongest," which means that the glory of only one equals the failure of all the rest. Participants not only over-valorize their own skills, but are confident of their strongholds. The stimulation of competition in the labor market, emulated by the entertainment industry, resulted in two interesting dynamics. On one hand, the industrial order faced what Robert Castel (2010) dubbed "the rise of uncertainty." The vulnerability of rank-and-file workers associated with the decline of welfare state facilitated the capital-owners to increase their profits and wealth; at the time, risk was adopted as a new value for modern workers. As Richard Sennett (2011) observed, the idea of risk implies that workers are co-managing their own fate; not only are they responsible for their decisions, but also this relieves the elite from their responsibility to create the conditions for a fairer wealth distribution. This gives capital further freedom to move worldwide. Paradoxically, on another hand, we, in terms of realism, are safer than in earlier cruel times, though audiences are bombarded by abstract risks. In this context, democracy is the legal and ideological platform that facilitates the expansion of late-capitalism. In ancient Greece, as Castoriadis (2006) widely demonstrated, democracy was a legal resource (which comes from *demos*) where lay-citizens can derogate a law if it was unjust or affected the interest of someone. Modern democracy, far from channeling rights in this direction, creates a gap between citizens and officials. This gap is fulfilled by trade and businesses corporations which financially support potential candidates for the presidency. Last but not least, Baudrillard (2006) is not wrong about his thesis of simulacra. While some policies are politically applied to solve some problems, policy-makers' real reasons are covered to protect the interests of the status quo. Risks are phantoms that keep the workforce immobile. As an example, Baudrillard (2006) brings into question the legitimacy of democracy by introducing the figure of "precogs" (in the film *Minority Report*). These agents worked jointly with police to forecast a crime before it is committed. As a result of this, police arrested the suspected criminal, not for what had been done, but for future crimes. This, to my end, is a brilliant and beautiful metaphor of how the modern world works—a point on which that Pinker and followers would think twice. Violence has declined in view of how reality has set the pace to pseudo-reality. The world painted by Pinker, where violence has been reduced to its minimum expression, still remains, with great inequalities between oppressors and the oppressed classes. Paradoxically, violence has been limited over the recent decades but not for the reasons stipulated in Pinker's argument. Innate to humans, violence and rivalry are two important factors to configure the cultural ethos under the binomial "enemy-friend." Whenever violence is curbed not only does the culture disappear, but also it corresponds with a valid indicator of submission, exploitation or control. History is witness to how Aboriginal great civilizations and empires collapsed when Spanish law forbade conducting the war against their neighbors. The notions of peace, mobilites and leisure are conducive to the empire order when, by means of pacification, it needs to exploit the resources of the periphery. The paradox lies in the fact that while violence has plummeted in our days, capitalism has show intself to be a productive machine that has caused serious inequalities worldwide. Whereas less violent, this world is very unjust for many workers.

# Bibliography

Acemoglu, D., & Robinson, J. (2012). *Why nations fail: The origins of power, prosperity and poverty*. New York, NY: Crown Publishing.

Adorno, T. W. (1997). *Aesthetic theory*. In R. Hullot-Kentor (Trans. and Ed.). Minneapolis, MN: University of Minnesota Press.

Anderson, D., & Grove, R. H. (1989). *Conservation in Africa: Peoples, policies and practice*. Cambridge: Cambridge University Press.

Aragonés-Estella, E. (2006). Visiones de tres diablos medievales. *De Arte*, 5, 15–27.

Ariès, P. (1975). *Western attitudes toward death: From the Middle Ages to the present* (Vol. 3). Maryland, VA: John Hopkins University Press.

Ariès, P. (2013). *The hour of our death*. New York, NY: Vintage.

Augé, M. (1995). *Non-places: An introduction to an anthropology of supermodernity* (trans. John Howe). New York, NY: Verso.

Augé, M. (1997). *L'impossible voyage: le tourisme et ses images*. Paris: Payot & Rivages.

Austen, R. A. (2010). The moral economy of witchcraft. In R. Grinker, S. Lubkemann, & C. Steiner (Eds.), *Perspectives on Africa: A reader in culture, history and representation* (pp. 270–273). Malden, MA: Willey-Blackwell.

Babones, S. (14 February 2012). «U.S. Income Distribution: Just How Unequal?». Inequality.org. http://inequality.org/unequal-americas-income-distribution/.

Bardis, P. D. (1981). *History of thanatology: Philosophical, religious, psychological, and sociological ideas concerning death, from primitive times to the present*. Washington, DC: University Press of America.

Baudrillard, J. (1985). Intellectual commitment and political power: An interview with Jean Baudrillard by Maria Shevtsova. *Thesis Eleven*.

Baudrillard, J. (1986). *America* (1–45). New York, New York: Verso.

Baudrillard, J. (1995a). *The Gulf War did not take place*. Sydney: Power Publications.

Baudrillard, J. (1995b). *The systems of the objects*. Mexico City: Siglo XXI.

Baudrillard, J. (1996). *The perfect crime*. London: Verso.

Baudrillard, J. (1997). Aesthetic illusion and virtual reality. In N. Zurbrugg (Ed.), *Jean Baudrillard: Art and Artefact* (19–27). New York, NY: Sage.

Baudrillard, J. (2000). *Pantalla total*. Barcelona: Anagrama.

Baudrillard, J. (2001). *Imposible exchange*. New York, NY: Verso.

Baudrillard, J. (2002). *Screened out*. New York, NY: Verso.

Baudrillard, J. (2003). *The spirit of terrorism*. New York, NY: Verso.

Baudrillard, J. (2006). Virtuality and events: The hell of power. *Baudrillard Studies*, 3(2).

Bauman, Z. (1998). *Globalization: The human consequences*. New York, NY: Columbia University Press.

Bauman, Z. (2007). *Consuming life*. Cambridge: Polity Press.

Bauman, Z. (2008). *Liquid fear*. Buenos Aires: Paidos.

Bauman, Z. (2011a). *Collateral damage: Social inequalities in a global age*. Cambridge: Polity Press.

Bauman, Z. (2011b). *La sociedad sitiada. [The besieged society]*. Buenos Aires: FCE..

Bauman, Z. (2013). *The individualized society*. New York, John Wiley & Sons.

Bauman, Z., & Lyon, D. (2013). *Liquid surveillance: A conversation*. New York, NY: John Wiley & Sons.

Beck, U. (1992). *Risk society: Towards a new modernity* (Vol. 17). London: Sage.

Beck, U. (2002). The terrorist threat world risk society revisited. *Theory, Culture & Society*, *19*(4), 39–55.

Beck, U. (2006). *La sociedad del riesgo: Hacia una nueva modernidad*. Buenos Aires: Paidos.

Beck, U. (2015). *Ecological politics in an age of risk*. New York, NY: John Wiley & Sons.

Benjamin, W. (1996). Critique of violence. In M. Bullock and M. W. Jennings (Eds.), *Walter Benjamin: Selected writings, volume I, 1913–1926* (pp. 236–252). Cambridge, MA: Belknap Press.

Benjamin, W. (2005). *The work of art in the age of mechanical reproduction*. Available online at http://www.marxists.org/reference/subject/philosophy/works/ge/benjamin.htm.

Berbeglia, E. (2002). Catastrofismo y control. In *Documental Laboris: Problemática actual de la psicología social* (pp. 179–195). Buenos Aires: Leuka.

Bernstein, R. (2006). *The abuse of evil: The corruption of politics and religión since 9/11*. Buenos Aires: Katz.

Bianchi, R. (2007). Tourism and the globalization of fear: Analyzing the politics of risk and (in)security in global travel. *Tourism and Hospitality Research 7*(1), 64–74.

Biocca, M. (2005). Risk communication and the precautionary principle. *Human and Ecological Risk Assessment: An International Journal*, *11*(1), 261–266.

Birtchnell, T., & Buscher, M. (2011). Stranded: An eruption of disruption. *Mobilities*, *6*(1), 1–9.

Bledstein, B. (1978). *The culture of professionalism: The middle class and the higher education in America*. New York: Norton.

Bowman, M. S., & Pezzullo, P. C. (2009). What's so "dark" about "dark tourism"? Death, tours, and performance. *Tourist Studies*, *9*(3), 187–202.

Brecht, B. (1964). *Brecht on theatre: The development of an aesthetic*. J. Willett (Trans. and Ed.). British edition. London: Methuen.

Bregha, F. (1989). Tourism, development, peace. *World Leisure & Recreation*, *31*(4), 5–8.

Brunsma, D., & Picou, J. S. (2008). Disasters in the twenty-first century: Modern destruction and future instruction. *Social Forces*, *87*(2), 983–991.

Bryant, W. C. (1817). Thanatopsis. *North American Review*, *5*(15), 338–341.

Bryant, W. C. (1948). The genesis of "Thanatopsis." *New England Quarterly*, *21* 163–184.

Buda, D. M., & McIntosh, A. J. (2013). Dark tourism and voyeurism: Tourist arrested for "spying" in Iran. *International Journal of Culture, Tourism and Hospitality Research*, *7*(3), 214–226.

Burley, M. (2008a). The B-theory of time and fear of death. *Polish Journal of Philosophy*, *2*(2), 21–38.

Burley, M. (2008b). Harry Silverstein's four dimensionalism and the perputed evil of death. *International Journal of Philosophical Studies*, *16*(4), 559–568.

Burley, M. (2010). Epicurus, death and the wrongness of killing. *Inquiry*, *53*(1), 68–86.

Campagne, F. A. (2009). *Strix Hispánica: Demonología cristiana y cultura folklórica en la España moderna*. Buenos Aires: Prometeo Libros.

Campbell, T. (2007). Poverty as a violation of human rights: Inhumanity or injustice? In T. Pogge (Ed.), *Freedom from poverty as a human right* (pp. 55–76). Oxford: Oxford University Press.

Castel, R. (2010). *El ascenso de las incertidumbres: trabajo, protecciones, estatuto del individuo.* Buenos Aires: Fondo de Cultura Económica.

Castoriadis, C. (2006). *Ce qui fait la Gréce.* Buenos Aires: Fondo de Cultura Económica.

Cohen, E. H. (2011). Educational dark tourism at an in populo site: The Holocaust museum in Jerusalem. *Annals of Tourism Research, 38*(1), 193–209.

Comaroff, J., & Comaroff, J. L. (1993). *Modernity and its malcontents: Ritual and power in postcolonial Africa.* Chicago, IL: University of Chicago Press.

Comaroff, J. L., & Comaroff, J. (2009). *Ethnicity, Inc.* Chicago, IL: University of Chicago Press.

Coulter, G. (2012). *Jean Baudrillard: From the ocean to the desert—The poetics of radicality.* Florida City, FL: Intertheory Press.

Deanesly, M. (1976). *A history of the medieval church: 590–1500.* London: Methuen.

Debord, G. (1967). *Society of the spectacle.* London: Bread and Circuses.

Degler, C. N. (1991). *In search of human nature: The decline and revival of Darwinism in American social thought.* Oxford: Oxford University Press.

De Vita, A. (2007) Inequality and poverty in global perspective? In T. Pogge (Ed.), *Freedom from poverty as a human right* (pp. 103–132). Oxford, Oxford University Press

Dick, P. K. (2002). The minority report. In *The minority report and other classic stories by Philp K. Dick.* New York, NY: Citadel Press. (Original work published 1956.)

Donohue, K. (2003). *Freedom from want.* Baltimore, MD: John Hopkins University.

Douglas, M. (2007). *Purity and danger: An analysis of concepts of pollution and taboo.* Buenos Aires: Nueva Visión.

Douglas, N. (1997). "The fearful and the fanciful: Early tourists perception in western Milanesia." *The Journal of Tourism Studies 8*(1), 52–60.

Durkheim, E. (1984). *The division of labor in society.* W. D. Halls (Trans.). New York, NY: The Free Press. (Original work published 1895.)

Dürr, E., & Jaffe, R. (2012). Theorizing slum tourism: Performing, negotiating and transforming inequality. *European Review of Latin American and Caribbean Studies/Revista Europea de Estudios Latinoamericanos y del Caribe, 5*(1), 113–123.

Dyson, P. (2012). Slum tourism: Representing and interpreting "reality" in Dharavi, Mumbai. *Tourism Geographies, 14*(2), 254–274.

Eliade, M. (2006). *The myth of eternal return.* Buenos Aires: Emece Editores.

Eliade, M. (2008). *Muerte y iniciaciones místicas.* Buenos Aires: Ed. Terramar.

Elías, N., & Dunning, E. (1992). *Deporte y ocio en el proceso de la civilización.* Buenos Aires: Fondo de Cultura Económica.

Esteva, G., & Prakash, M. S. (1998). Beyond development, what? *Development in Practice, 8*(3), 280–296.

Evans-Pritchard, E. E. (1977). Witchcraft (mangu) amongst the A-Zande. *Sudan Notes and Records, 3*(2), 163–249.

Ezzy, D. (2006). White witches and black magic: Ethics and consumerism in contemporary witchcraft. *Journal of Contemporary Religion, 21*(1), 15–31.

Fielding, R. et al. (2005). Avian influenza risk perception, Hong Kong. *Emerging Infectious Diseases, 11*(5), 677–682.

Fleurbaey, M. (2007). Poverty as a form of oppression. In T. Pogge (Ed.), *Freedom from poverty as a human right* (pp. 133–154). Oxford: Oxford University Press.

Foley, M., & Lennon, J. J. (1996). JFK and dark tourism: A fascination with assassination. *International Journal of Heritage Studies, 2*(4), 198–211.

Foucault, M. (1969). *L'archéologie du savoir*. Paris: Gallimard.

Foucault, M. (2007). *Birth of biopolitics*. Buenos Aires: FCE.

Foucault, M. (2009). Security, territory, population: Lectures at the Collège de France 1977–1978 (Vol. 4). New York, Macmillan.

Freire-Medeiros, B. (2014). *Touring poverty*. Abingdon: Routledge.

Freud, S. (1920). *Beyond the pleasure principle*, London: International Psycho-Analytical Press.

Frenzel, F., & Koens, K. (2012). Slum tourism: Developments in a young field of interdisciplinary tourism research. *Tourism Geographies*, *14*(2), 195–212.

Frenzel, F., Koens, K., Steinbrink, M., & Rogerson, M. (2014). Slum tourism: State of the art. *Tourism Review International*, *18*(4), 237–252.

Friedman, M. (1982). *Capitalism and freedom*. Chicago, IL: University of Chicago Press.

Fuchs, G., & Reichel, A. (2004). Cultural differences in tourist destination risk perception: an exploratory study. *Tourism (Zagreb)*, *52*(1), 21–37.

Gebauer, G., & Wulf, C. (2009). After the death of Man, from philosophical anthropology to historical anthropology. *Iris*, *1*(1), 171–186.

George, B., Inbakan, R., & Poyyamoli, G. (2010). To travel or not to travel: Towards understanding the theory of nativistic motivation. *Tourism: An International Interdisciplinary Journal*, *58*(4), 395–407.

Giddens, A. (1991). *Modernity and self-identity: Self and society in the late modern age*. Stanford, CA: Stanford University Press.

Giddens, A. (1999a). *Consecuencias de la modernidad*. Madrid: Alianza Editorial.

Giddens, A. (1999b). Risk and responsibility. *The Modern Law Review*, *62*(1), 1–10.

Giddens, A. (2000). *Un mundo desbocado: Los efectos de la globalización en nuestras vidas*. Madrid: Taurus.

González-Marín, C. (2005). Las mujeres y el mal. *Azafea*, 7: 119–129. Salamanca: Ediciones Universidad de Salamanca.

Graphs.net. (2013). *Vampires on social media*. Available online at http://www.graphs. net/201301/vampires-on-social-media.html.

Grossman, M. (2014). *Artists of the possible: Governing networks and American policy change since 1945*. Oxford: Oxford University Press.

Guidotti-Hernández, N. (2011). *Unspeakable violence: Remapping US and Mexican national imaginaries*. Durham, NC: Duke University Press.

Hannam, K., & Knox, D. (2005). Discourse analysis in tourism research: A critical perspective. *Tourism Recreation Research*, *30*(2), 23–30.

Hanson, M. (2008). *Economic development, education and transnational corporations*. Abingdon: Routledge.

Harvey, D. (1989). *The condition of postmodernity* (Vol. 14). Oxford: Blackwell.

Hawkins, M. (1997). *Social Darwinism in European and American thought, 1860–1945: Nature as model and nature as threat*. Cambridge: Cambridge University Press.

Heilbroner, R. L. (1995). *The worldly philosophers: The lives, times and ideas of the great economic thinkers*. New York, NY: Touchtone.

Hitchens, C. (2012). *The missionary position: Mother Teresa in theory and practice*. New York, NY: Twelve.

Hobbes, T. (1998). *Leviathan*. México: Fondo de Cultura Económica. (Original work published 1651.)

Hobsbawm, E. (1994). *The age of extremes: A history of the world 1914–1991*. New York, NY: Vintage.

Hofstadter, R. (1963). *Anti-intellectualism in American life*. New York, NY: Vintage.

Hofstadter, R. (1992). *Social Darwinism in American thought*. Boston, MA: Beacon Press. (Original work published 1944.)

Holst, T. (2014). Touring the demolished slum? Slum tourism in the face of Delhi's gentrification. *Tourism Review International, 18*(4), 283–294.

Ingold, T. (2011). *Being alive: Essays on movement knowledge and description*. London: Routledge.

Jafari, J. (1989). Tourism and peace. *Annals of Tourism Research, 16*(3), 439–443.

Jameson, F. (1991). *Postmodernism, or the cultural logic of late capitalism*. Durham, NC: Duke University Press.

Jameson, F. (2002). The dialectics of disaster. *The South Atlantic Quarterly, 101*(2), 297–304.

Jenkins, M. (2008). Time for Leviathan? *Philosophy Pathways*, Vol. 18. Available online at www.philosophypathways.com.

Johnston, T. (2013). Mark Twain and *The Innocents Abroad*: Illuminating the tourist gaze on death. *International Journal of Culture and Hospitality Research, 7*(3), 199–213.

Kaelber, L. (2007). A memorial as virtual trauma-escape: Darkest tourism in 3D and cyber space to the gas chambers of Auschwitz. *E-Review of Tourism Research, 5*(2), 24–33

Karlsen, C. (1987). *The devil in the shape of a woman: Witchcraft in colonial New England*. New York, NY: W. W. Norton & Company.

Kellner, D. (2005). Baudrillard, globalization and terrorism: Some comments in recent adventures of the image and spectable on the occasion of Baudrillard's 75th birthday. *Baudrillard Studies, 2*(1), 1–17.

Klein, N. (2007). *The shock doctrine: The rise of disaster capitalism*. New York, NY: Macmillan.

Kohnert, D. (1996). Magic and witchcraft: Implications for democratization and poverty-alleviating aid in Africa. *World Development, 24*(8), 1347–1355.

Korstanje, M. E. (2009). Re-visiting risk perception theory in the context of travel. *E-Review of Tourism Research, 7*(4), 68–81.

Korstanje, M. E. (2010). Commentaries on our new ways of perceiving disasters. *Disaster Resilience in the Built Environment, 1*(2), 241–248.

Korstanje, M. E. (2011a). Detaching the elementary forms of dark-tourism. *Anatolia, 22*(3), 424–427.

Korstanje, M. E. (2011b) Rebelión: Una aproximación teórica. *International Journal of Žižek Studies, 5*(4), 1–43.

Korstanje, M. E. (2011c). Reconnecting with poverty: New challenges of disaster management. *International Journal of Disaster Resilience in the Built Environment, 2*(2), 165–177.

Korstanje, M. E. (2011d). Swine flu in Buenos Aires: Beyond the principle of resilience. *International Journal of Disaster Resilience in the Built Enviroment, 2*(1), 59–73.

Korstanje, M. E. (2012). Reconsidering cultural tourism: An anthropologist's perspective. *Journal of Heritage Tourism, 7*(2), 179–184.

Korstanje, M. E. (2013). Review of Olympic ceremonialism and the performance of national character. *Event Management* 17, 453–455.

Korstanje, M. E. (2014a). Chile helps Chile: Exploring the effects of earthquake Chile 2010. *International Journal of Disaster Resilience in the Built Environment, 5*(4), 380–390.

Korstanje, M. E. (2014b). Dark tourism and place identity: Managing and interpreting dark places (contemporary geographies of leisure, tourism and mobility). *Journal of Tourism and Cultural Change, 12*(4), 369–371.

Korstanje, M. E. (2014c). Why risk-research is more prominent in English speaking countries in the digital society. *International Journal of Cyber Warfare and Terrorism, 4*(1), 8–18.

Korstanje M. E. (2015). *A difficult world: Examining the roots of capitalism.* New York, NY: Nova Science.

Korstanje, M. E. (2016). El diseño del capitalismo mortuorio: De la cultura del desastre al narcisismo. *Reflexiones Marginales, 32,* 1–19.

Korstanje M. E., & Busby, G. (2010). Understanding the Bible as the roots of physical displacement: The origin of tourism. *E-Review of Tourism Research, 8*(3), 95–111.

Korstanje, M. E., & Clayton, A. (2012). Tourism and terrorism: Conflicts and commonalities. *Worldwide Hospitality and Tourism Themes, 4*(1), 8–25.

Korstanje, M. E., & George, B. (2015). Dark Tourism: Revisiting Some Philosophical Issues. *E-review of Tourism Research, 12* (1–2):127–136.

Korstanje, M. E., & Ivanov, S. (2012). Tourism as a form of new psychological resilience: The inception of dark tourism. *Cultur: Revista de Cultura e Turismo, 6*(4), 56–71.

Korstanje M. E., & Skoll, G. (2012). Risk totems and fetishes in Marx and Freud. *Sincronia, 1*(1), 1–20.

Korstanje, M. E., & Tarlow, P. (2012). Being lost: Tourism, risk and vulnerability in the post-"9/11" entertainment industry. *Journal of Tourism and Cultural Change, 10*(1), 22–33.

Korstanje, M. E., Tzanelli, R., & Clayton, A. (2014). Brazilian World Cup 2014: Terrorism, tourism, and social conflict. *Event Management, 18*(4), 487–491.

Kuhn, T. S. (1962). Historical structure of scientific discovery. *Science, 136*(3518), 760–764.

Larsen, S. (2007). Aspects of a psychology of the tourist experience. *Scandinavian Journal of Hospitality and Tourism, 7*(1), 7–18.

Larsen, S. (2009). What tourists worry about: Construction of a scale measuring tourist worries. *Tourism Management, 30*(1), 260–265.

Lasch, C. (1991). *The culture of narcissism.* New York, NY: WW Norton & Company.

Lash, S., & Urry, J. (1998). *Economías de signo y espacio: Sobre el capitalismo de la postorganización.* Buenos Aires: Amorrortu Editores.

Lazar, S. (2012). How zombies became a social-media firebomb. *Entrepreneur* 8 March 2012. Available online at http://www.entrepreneur.com/blog/223075.

Leach, E. (1954). *Political systems of highland Burma: A study of Kachin social structure.* London: Editorial Bell.

Leach, E. (1965). *Lévi-Strauss, antropólogo y filósofo.* Barcelona: Anagrama.

Lears, J. (1994). *No place of grace: Antimodernism and the transformation of American culture, 1880–1920.* Chicago, IL: University of Chicago Press.

LeBaron, E. (2014). Re-imagining the geography of the Favelas: Pacification, tourism and transformation in Complexo Do Alemão, Rio de Janeiro. *Tourism Review International, 18*(4), 269–282.

Lemke, T. (2001). "The birth of bio-politics": Michel Foucault's lecture at the College de France on neo-liberal governmentality. *Economy and Society, 30*(2), 190–207.

Lennon, J., & Foley, M. (2000). *Dark tourism: The attraction of death and disasters.* London: Thomson Learning.

Lévi-Strauss, C. (1991). *The elementary structures of kinship.* Madrid: Paidos.

Lévi-Strauss, C. (1995). *Structural anthropology.* Buenos Aires: Ediciones Paidos.

Lévi-Strauss, C. (2002). *Myth and meaning.* Madrid: Editorial Alianza.

Lévi-Strauss, C. (2003). *The savage mind.* México: FCE.

Lew, A. (1987). A framework of tourist attraction research. *Annals of Tourism Research, 14*(4), 553–575.

Litvin, S. W. (1998). Tourism: The world's peace industry? *Journal of Travel Research, 37*(1): 63–66.

Luhmann, N. (1990). Technology, environment and social risk: A systems perspective. *Organization & Environment, 4*(3), 223–231.

Luhmann, N. (2006). *Sociología del riesgo*. México: Universidad Iberoamericana.

MacCannell, D. (2003). *The tourist: A new theory of leisure class*. Moia, Spain: Ed. Melusina.

MacKendrick, K. (2009). Evil in world religion at the University of Manitoba (2002–2008): An introduction and provocation. *Golem, 3*(1), 38–55.

Maffesoli, M. (2003). *L'instant éternel: Le retour du tragique dans les sociétés postmodernes*. Paris: La Table Ronde.

Malinowski, B. (1998). *Estudios de psicología primitiva*. Buenos Aires: Editorial Altaya.

Markale, J. (2006). *Les revoltes de Dieu*. Buenos Aires: Ateneo.

Marx, K. (1967). *Capital: Volume 1, the process of capitalist production*. F. Engels (Ed.). New York, NY: International Publishers. (Original work published 1867.)

Marx, K. (1973). *Grundrisse: Foundations of the critique of political economy*. M. Nicolaus (Trans). Harmondsworth and New York, NY: Penguin Books. (Original work published 1939).

Marx, L. (1994). The idea of technology and postmodern pessimism. In Y. Ezrahi, E. Mendelsohn, & H. Segal (Eds.), *Technology, pessimism, and postmodernism* (pp. 11–28). Dordrecht: Kluwer Academic Publishers.

McClintock, A. (2013). *Imperial leather: Race, gender, and sexuality in the colonial contest*. New York, NY: Routledge.

McLuhan, M., & Fiore, Q. (1967). The medium is the message. *New York, 123,* 126–128.

McMichael, P. (2012). *Development and social change*. 5th edition. Thousand Oaks, CA: Sage.

Mead, G. H. (2009). *Mind, self, and society: From the standpoint of a social behaviourist* (Vol. 1). Chicago, IL: University of Chicago Press.

Mekawy, M. (2014). Smart tourism investment: Planning pathways to break the poverty cycle. *Tourism Review International, 18*(4), 253–268.

Merleau-Ponty, M. (1964). *Sense and non-sense*. Illinois, IL: Northwestern University Press.

Meschkank, J. (2011). Investigations into slum tourism in Mumbai: Poverty tourism and the tensions between different constructions of reality. *GeoJournal, 76*(1), 47–62.

Michaud, Y. (2013). *Le nouveau luxe: Expériences, arrogance, authenticité*. Paris: Stock.

Michaud, Y. (2015). *El nuevo lujo: Experiencias, arrogancia y autenticidad*. Buenos Aires: Taurus.

Middleton, J. (Ed.). (1967). *Magic, witchcraft, and curing*. Garden City, New York, NY: Natural History Press.

Morris, Bryan. (1995). La interpretación de los símbolos. In *Introducción al estudio antropológico de la religión*. Barcelona: Paidos.

Muchembled, R. (2000). *Historia del diablo, siglos XII–XX*. Buenos Aires: FCE.

O'Rourke, P. J. (1988). *Holidays in hell*. London: Picador Ed.

Oster, E. (2004). Witchcraft, weather and economic growth in Renaissance Europe. *Journal of Economic Perspectives, 18*(1), 215–228.

Patterson, J. T. (1994). *America's struggle against poverty, 1900–1994*. Cambridge, MA: Harvard University Press.

Pfau, A. (2013). Ritualized violence against sorcerers in fifteenth-century France. *Magic, Ritual, and Witchcraft. 8*(1), 50–72.

Pilger, J. (2013). *The new propaganda is liberal—the new slavery is digital*. (13 March 2016). Available online at http://johnpilger.com/articles/the-new-propaganda-is-liberal-the-new-slavery-is-digital.

Pinker, S. (2011). *The better angels of our nature: Why violence has declined*. New York, NY: Penguin.

Pippin, R. (1994). On the notion of technology as ideology: Prospects. In Y. Ezrahi, E. Mendelsohn, & H. Segal (Eds.), *Technology, pessimism, and post-modernism* (pp. 93–113). Dordrecht: Kluwer Academic Publishers.

Pizam, A. (1996). Does tourism promote peace and understanding between unfriendly nations? In *Tourism, crime and international security issues* (pp. 203–213). New York: Wiley & Sons.

Pogge, T. (2007). Introduction. In T. Pogge (Ed.), *Freedom from poverty as a human right* (pp. 1–11). Oxford: Oxford University Press,

Poria, Y. (2007). Establishing cooperation between Israel and Poland to save Auschwitz concentration camp: Globalising the responsibility for the massacre. *International Journal of Tourism Policy*, *1*(1), 45–57.

Quarantelli, E. L. (1960). A note on the protective function of the family in disasters. *Marriage and Family Living*, *22*(3), 263–264.

Quarantelli, E. L. (2006). The disasters of the 21st century: A mixture of new, old, and mixed types. *Disaster Research Center*, Preliminary Paper 353. Newark, DE: University of Delaware.

Rae, W. (2008). A prevalence of witches: Witchcraft and popular culture in the Making of a Yoruba town. *Journal of Religion and Popular Culture*. Vol. 18. Article 18. Available online at 222.usask.ca/relst/jrpc/18-witches.

Rajan, K. S. (2007). *Bio-capital: The constitution of postgenomic life*. Durham: Duke University Press.

Rajan, R. (2010). *Fault lines: How hidden fractures still threaten the world economy*. Princeton, NJ: Princeton University Press.

Rawls, J. (1993). The law of peoples. *Critical Inquiry*, *20*(1), 36–68.

Rawls, J. (2001). *The law of peoples, with, "The idea of public reason revisited."* Cambridge, MA: Harvard University Press.

Reijinders, S. (2009). Watching the detectives inside the guilty landscapes of Inspector Morse, Baantjer and Wallander. *European Journal of Communication*, *24*(2), 165–181.

Riesman, D. (1953). *The lonely crowd: A study of the changing American character* (Vol. 16). New York, NY: Doubleday.

Rifkin, J. (1998). *The biotech century*. New York: Jeremy P. Tarcher/Putnam.

Rojek, C. (1997). Indexing, dragging and the social construction of tourist sights. In C. Rojek & J. Urry (Eds.), *Touring cultures: Transformations of travel and theory* (pp. 52–74). London: Routledge.

Roubini, N., & Setser, B. (2004). *Bailouts or bail-ins? Responding to financial crises in emerging economies*. Washington, DC: Institute for International Economics.

Russell, F. H. (1977). *The just war in the Middle Ages*. Cambridge: Cambridge University Press.

Russell, J. B. (1986). *Lucifer: The devil in the Middle Ages*. Ithaca, NY: Cornell University Press.

Ryan, C. (2005). "Dark Tourism—An introduction." In C. Ryan, S. Page, & M. Aitlen (187–190). *Taking tourism to the limits: Issues, concepts and managerial perspectives*. Oxford: Elsevier.

Ryan, W. (1971). *Blaming the victims*. New York: Vintage Books.

Sather-Wagstaff, J. (2011). *Heritage that hurts: Tourists in the memoryscapes of September 11* (Vol. 4). Thousands Oaks, CA: Left Coast Press.

Schuster, H. (2006). El mal: una mirada desde la reflexión filosófica o la lucidez descifradora no necesariamente es un bien. *Revista de Filosofía*, 15, 201–217.

Seaton, A. V. (1996). Guided by the dark: From thanatopsis to thana-tourism. *International Journal of Heritage Studies*, *2*(4), 234–244.

Seaton, A. V. (1999). War and thanatourism: Waterloo 1815–1914. *Annals of Tourism Research*, *26*(1), 130–158.

Seaton, A. V. (2000). Thanatourism: Entry. In J. Jafari (Ed.), *Encyclopedia of Tourism* (1–7). London: Routledge.

Sennett, R. (2011). *The corrosion of character: The personal consequences of work in the new capitalism*. New York, NY: WW Norton & Company.

Sharpley, R. (2005). Travels to the edge of darkness: Towards a typology of dark tourism. In C. Ryan, S. Page, & M. Aicken (Eds.), *Taking tourism to the limits: Issues, concepts and managerial perspectives* (217–228). Oxford: Elsevier.

Skinner, J. (2012). *Writing the dark side of travel*. New York, NY: Berghan Books.

Skoll, G. (2010). *Social theory of fear*. New York, NY: Palgrave Macmillan.

Skoll, G. (2014). *Dialectics in social thought*. New York, NY: Palgrave Macmillan.

Skoll, G. (2016). *Globalization of American fear culture: The empire in the twenty-first century*. New York, NY: Palgrave Macmillan.

Skoll, G. R., & Korstanje, M. E. (2012). Risks, totems, and fetishes in Marx and Freud. *Sincronía*, (2), 11–27.

Skoll, G. R., & Korstanje, M. E. (2013). Constructing an American fear culture from red scares to terrorism. *International Journal of Human Rights and Constitutional Studies*, *1*(4), 341–364.

Sojberg, L. (1999). Risk perception by the public and by experts: A dilemma in risk management. *Human Ecology Review 6*(2), 1–9.

Soyinka, W. (2005). *The climate of fear: The quest for dignity in dehumanized world*. New York, NY: Random House.

Starr, P. (1982). *The social transformation of American medicine*. New York, NY: Basic Books.

Stiglitz, J. (2003). *Globalization and its discontents*. New York, NY: W. W. Norton & Company.

Stone, P. (2005). Dark tourism consumption—A call for research. *E-Review of Tourism Research* 3 (5), 109–117.

Stone, P. (2006). A dark tourism spectrum: Towards a typology of death and macabre related tourist sites, attraction and exhibitions. *Tourism*, *54*(2), 145–160.

Stone, P. (2011). Dark tourism and the cadaveric carnival: Mediating life and death narratives at Gunther Von Hagens' Body Worlds. *Current Issues in Tourism*, *14*(7), 681–701.

Stone, P. (2012). Dark tourism as mortality capital. *Annals of Tourism Research*, *39*(3), 1565–1587.

Stone, P., & Sharpley, R. (2008). Consuming dark tourism: A thanatological perspective. *Annals of Tourism Research*, *35*(2), 574–595.

Stout, H. (1986). *The New England soul*. Oxford: Oxford University Press.

Strange, C., & Kempa, M. (2003). Shades of dark tourism: Alcatraz and Robben Island. *Annals of Tourism Research*, *30*(2), 386–405.

Sunstein, C. R. (2002a). Probability neglect: Emotions, worst cases, and law. *The Yale Law Journal*, *112*(1) 61–107.

Sunstein, C. R. (2002b). *Risk and reason: Safety, law, and the environment*. Cambridge: Cambridge University Press.

Takaki, R. (1990). *Iron cages: Race and culture in 19th century America*. Oxford: Oxford University Press.

Tang, C., & Wong, K. N. (2009). The SARS epidemic and international visitors arrivals to Cambodia: Is the impact permanent or transitory? *Tourism Economics*, *15*(4), 883–890.

Tarlow, P. (2014). *Tourism security: Strategies for effectively managing travel risk and safety*. Oxford: Elsevier.

Taylor-Gooby, P. F. (2004). *New risks, new welfare: The transformation of the European welfare state*. Oxford: Oxford University Press.

Thomas, K. V. (1978). *Religion and the decline of magic*. London: Penguin.

Thurow, L. C. (2001). *The zero-sum society: Distribution and the possibilities for economic change*. New York, NY: Basic Books.

Tzanelli, R. (2011). *Cosmopolitan memory in Europe's backwaters*. Abingdon: Routledge.

Tzanelli, R. (2014). Embodied art and aesthetic performativity in the London 2012 handover to Rio (2016). *Global Studies Journal, 6*(2), 13–24.

Tzanelli, R. (2015a). On *Avatar's* (2009) semiotechnologies: From cinematic utopias to Chinese heritage tourism. *Tourism Analysis, 20*(3), 269–282.

Tzanelli, R. (2015b). *Socio-cultural mobility and mega-events: Ethics and aesthetics in Brazil 2014 World Cup*. Abingdon: Routledge.

Tzanelli, R. (2016). *Thana tourism and the cinematic representation of risk*. Abingdon: Routledge.

Urry, J. (November 2001). Globalizing the tourist-gaze. Proceedings *from Cityscapes Conference. Graz, Austria.*

Urry, J. (2002). *The tourist gaze*. London: Sage.

Urry, J. (2007). Introducción, culturas móviles In P. Zusman, C. Lois, & H. Castro (Eds.), *En viajes y geografías* (17–31). Buenos Aires: Prometeo.

Veblen, T. (1899). *The theory of the leisure class*. New York, NY: Macmillan.

Verma, S., & Jain, R. (2013). Exploiting tragedy for tourism. *Research on Humanities and Social Sciences, 3*(8), 9–13.

Virilio, P. (1991). *La inseguridad del territorio*. Buenos Aires: La Marca.

Virilio, P. (1996). *El arte del motor: Aceleración y realidad*. Buenos Aires: Ediciones el Manantial.

Virilio, P. (2003). *Art and fear*. Rose (Trans). New York, NY: Continuum.

Virilio, P. (2007). *Ciudad pánico: El afuera comienza aquí*. Buenos Aires: Libros el Zorzal.

Virilio, P. (2010). *The university of disaster*. Oxford: Polity Press.

Walter, T. (2009). Dark tourism: Mediating between the dead and the living. In R. Sharpley & P. Stone (Eds.) *The darker side of travel: The theory and practice of dark tourism* (39–55). Bristol: Channel View Publications.

Weber, M. (1958). *Essays in sociology*. New York, NY: Oxford University Press.

Weber, M. (2002). *The Protestant ethic and the spirit of Capitalism: And other writings*. New York, NY: Penguin Books. (Original work published 1930.)

Weiner, A. B. (1985). Inalienable wealth. *American Ethnologist, 12*(2), 210–227.

Weiner, A. B. (1992). *Inalienable possessions: The paradox of keeping-while giving*. Berkeley, CA: University of California Press.

Weinrib, E. (1995). *The idea of private law*. Cambridge, MA: Harvard University Press.

Wenge, C. (2007). Razones para Viajar. *Factótum: Revista de Filosofía, 5,* 88–91. Edición Viajes y Viajeros. Available online at http://www.revistafactotum.com/.

White, L., & Frew, E. (2013). *Dark tourism and place identity: Managing and interpreting dark places*. London: Routledge.

Wilby, E. (2013). Buchard's strigae, the witches Sabbath, and shamanistic cannibalism in early modern Europe. *Magic, Ritual, and Witchcraft, 8*(1), 18–49.

Yuill, S. M. (2004). *Dark tourism: Understanding visitor motivation at sites of death and disaster* (Doctoral dissertation, Texas A&M University).

Žižek, S. (2003). *The puppet and the dwarf: The perverse core of Christianity*. Cambridge, MA: MIT Press.

Žižek, S. (2011). El estado de emergencia económica permanente. *A diez años del 11 de Septiembre: Cómo cambió el mundo* (pp. 203–208). Edición Le Monde Diplomatiqué. Buenos Aires: Capital Intellectual.

Žižek, S. (2016). Is God dead, unconsciouss, evil, impotent, stupid … or just counterfactual? *International Journal of Žižek Studies, 10*(1), 1–31.

# Index